Dedication

This book is dedicated to my father-in-law Herman Page. The restoration of the Villa Real would not have happened without his infectious love of Pullman cars and his financial support. It is also dedicated to my wife, Lois. She maintained the home, provided moral support, and tolerated the constant parade of railroad car parts that filled our garage for twenty-six years.

About the author: Al Sauer grew up in western Kansas and was always fascinated by trains. That fascination flourished after meeting his future father-in-law, Herman Page whose passion for Pullman Cars was highly contagious. An electrical engineer, Albuilt his career through employment with Motorola, Memorex-Telex, Intergraph, IBM, Elster American Meter and Lenovo. Working and living in Huntsville Alabama in 1991 he joined the North Alabama Railroad Museum where he helped restore an S-2 Alco locomotive, an Ingersol-Rand Boxcab locomotive, and 3 passenger cars during six active years. He and Herman acquired the Villa Real in 1995. Al and the car moved to Raleigh, North Carolina in 1998, following a job change. Retirement in 2018 allowed him to concentrate on completing the Villa Real's restoration.

Authors Note: When Herman Page and I acquired the Villa Real, I seriously underestimated the amount of work and time required to complete a restoration. The intent was always to restore the car to how it looked in 1931. It was never intended to become a private car to be pulled on Amtrak. I originally estimated the work could be completed in about six years. Over the years, friends would ask "When will it be done?" and I would jokingly respond, "about 6 years." That response did not change until I retired and could actually see the light at the end of the tunnel twenty-six and one half years later.

I always intended for the car to be displayed in a museum when the restoration was finished. The Illinois Railway Museum was the best choice because it had sufficient indoor exhibit space to house the car and would run the car on special occasions. People have asked me "Won't you miss it?" Actually, the answer is "Not really." I found joy in doing the restoration: the research, finding and making parts, solving problems, and finishing the car.

Keeping the Villa was not the plan. I also never intended to write a book. I was taking a lot of photos during the restoration to create a scrap book. Only recently, I realized that there were some good stories to go along with the before, during and after photos. I hope you have as much fun reading about and seeing the journey as I did taking the journey.

All rights reserved. No part of this book may be reproduced in any form or by any means, except for the inclusion of brief quotations for review purposes, without the written permission of the publisher.

ISBN: 978-0-578-37575-5

First Printing 2022

Copyright © 2022 by Albert Sauer

All Rights reserved

Table of Contents

History of the Villa Real 3
The Acquisition 7
Villa Real Restoration Summary 9
Exterior Wall Steel 11
Exterior Paint History 15
Clover Lodge 17
Buffer Plates and Curtains 21
Move from Huntsville to Raleigh 24
Electricity 26
Exterior Paint – Round 1 30
Wheel and Bearing Swap 35
Men's Room Wall and Couch 41
Men's Room Floor Failure 48
Vestibules and Steps 51
Dutch Doors and Traps 58
The Trap Doors 62
Section Area 63
Light Fixtures 75
Fans 78
New Upholstery 80
Interior Paint 81
Ladies' Room 87
Roof Steel 94
Window Steel 98
Long Hallway 102
Bedroom Hoppers 108
Bedrooms 114
3D Printing 119
Vinyl Flooring 123
Window Sash Restoration 126
Faux Woodgrain Finish 138
The Porter Call Box 144
Exterior Paint – Round 2 146
Carpet 148
Raleigh to Illinois Railway Museum Move 151
The Final Result 155

History of the Villa Real

On March 21, 1911, the Pullman-Standard Car Manufacturing Company completed the 12 section, 1 drawing room, 1 compartment sleeping car Lenover, Plan 2411, Lot 3880, for general service in the Pullman fleet. The construction of steel cars was encouraged by the management of the Pennsylvania Railroad, which expressed concern over operation of wooden cars in the newly completed tunnels between New Jersey and Penn Station. Lenover was one in a series of eight cars all of which sacrificed lavatory space for the sake of the compartment that was squeezed into a standard 12 section, 1 double bedroom, and 1 drawing room floor plan. Attired in Tuscan red and lettered "Pullman," the car was assigned to the Pennsylvania Railroad.

The Pullman photo of a 12-1-1 sleeper from the series

The car was upgraded in 1920 to new brakes and trucks. It was also painted in standard Pullman green color, but that only lasted for one year when the car was returned to Tuscan red. It continued in Pennsylvania Railroad service until Pullman converted it to a 10 section, 3 double bedroom car in January 1931 and renamed it the Villa Real.

As the demand for more private room space increased, Pullman responded by rebuilding and reconfiguring many existing standard sleeping cars of the era. Sometimes the rebuilding effort was referred to as a 'betterment' program.

As for the Villa Real, the drawing room, double bedroom and two sections were removed and replaced with three double bedrooms. The women's lavatory was enlarged and became the men's smoking room and lavatory. The existing men's lavatory became the women's room. The rebuilding work on Villa Real was done at the Pullman shops near Chicago along with thirty-five other cars rebuilt with the same 3411 floor plan. They were all renamed in the Villa series.

Villa Real remained assigned to the Pennsylvania Railroad but was painted in Pullman green with gold lettering like the rest of the Pullman fleet on January 14, 1931. However, air conditioning was in its infancy in 1931 and Villa Real was one of eight (of thirty-six) rebuilt cars in the Villa Series that had not been so equipped. As the years wore on its non-air-conditioned status made the car less desirable for travelers and railroads alike.

Occasionally, Villa Real would make it to St. Louis for repairs and slight adjustments. A balky berth lock might be repaired at the Jefferson Avenue Yard by the Pullman staff at 21st Street. Electrical problems or heavier maintenance such as truck pedestal

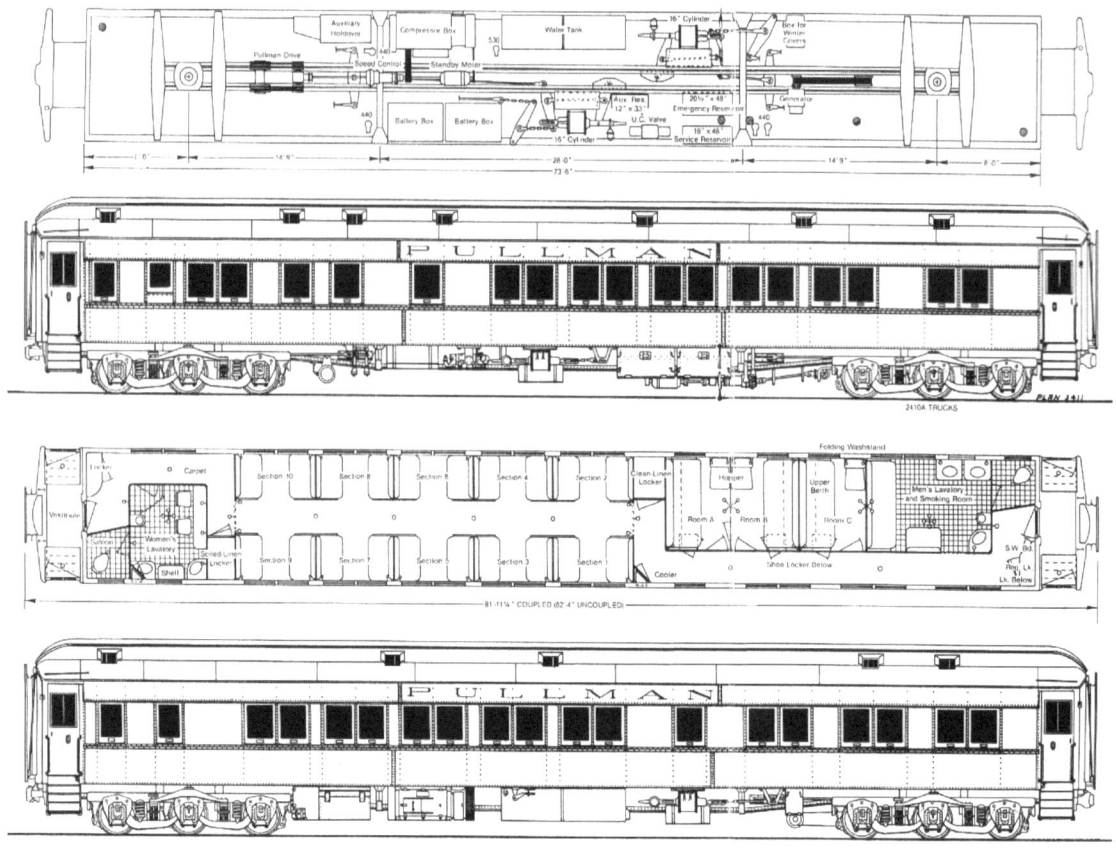

Pullman Plan 3411

replacement would require the car to be taken to the Pullman Company repair shops on the Terminal Railroad Association's West Belt a few blocks from Shreve Avenue at 5550 Bircher Street. Villa Real visited these shops in 1934, 1936, 1939, 1945 and 1947, for wiring work and similar minor repairs.

After the 1949 breakup of the Pullman Company into separate car building and car leasing companies, the sleeping cars were sold to the rail lines and then leased back to Pullman for operation. Some cars remained unsold due to their non-air-conditioned status or the undesirability of their room accommodations. These unsold cars remained in the now shrinking Pullman pool which provided large numbers of cars upon demand for conventions, troop movements, Boy Scout jamborees and similar large crowd functions.

In November 1950 Villa Real arrived in St. Louis for storage, but in February 1951 was sent to the Pullman shops at Buffalo for renumbering and assignment to tourist service as Tourist Car 5141. Tourist service was a term used to describe cars, all of which were non-air-conditioned, and utilized to provide a low cost means of transporting large numbers of people. The primary service was troop transport for the Korean War. As the Korean War needs diminished, Villa Real was once again available for other assignments. Tourist cars were also used to attract large numbers of family travelers and vacationers looking for inexpensive transportation.

For conversion to tourist service many of the normal fittings and décor, such as carpeting, berth lights, and other items were removed. The movable walls between Bedrooms A and B were taken out, and the toilet-wash stands were removed from all the bedrooms, along with the doors opening into the hallway. The berths in the former bedrooms were sold as sections or uppers and lowers.

Mexico City - Guadalajara Service

Villa Real was in service in Mexico in the late 1930's; the car was found to be listed in a timetable during that time. Shop records in Atlanta in 1941, indicate that it was returned to the United States prior to the country's entry into World War II. The car was sold on October 16, 1953, to the Wabash Railroad with Villa Real, now Pullman Tourist 5141, becoming the Wabash 4318. An examination of the paint on the outside of the car revealed that it had been sandblasted and repainted by the Wabash. The bottom layer of paint is Tuscan red with white lettering that reads "Wabash". Wabash "Flag" emblems over each wheel set indicated that it continued in regular passenger service. The car was then leased back to Pullman to continue in its passenger car operating business. Pullman had little use in the U.S. for a non-air-conditioned car. So, it went to Guadalajara, Mexico. The Pullman porters and conductors hired in Mexico were Pullman employees, and were expected to uphold company wide Pullman standards.

Mexican tickets, business card and Coins found in the razor blade repository

Maintenance of Way Service (MoW)

In June 1957, Wabash once again took possession of the car. It was then that the Wabash railroad converted the car into a wreck train's foreman's car at the Decatur, Illinois shops. There the car was painted MoW silver but kept the same 4318 number, as Wabash floor plan drawings document. The lettering was painted safety red.

The wall between Bedrooms A and B was removed. These two adjacent bedrooms became the foreman's office and bedroom; the wall between the men's room and bedroom C was removed to expand the men's room and make room for a shower and wall lockers. Three of the sections were removed to make room to house an oil burning furnace, and duct work was cut into the walls and hung just under the ceiling to provide forced air heating to all areas of the car. The two windows in the toilets, the one-paired section window immediately in front of the furnace and the window from the former section were plated over on the outside. Steel was welded over the doorway to bedrooms C. The three original porcelain sinks in the men's room were left intact.

4318 continued as a wrecker foreman's car after the Wabash merger in 1964 with the Norfolk and Western Railway and was renumbered 564318. It retained that number until it was retired in 1994.

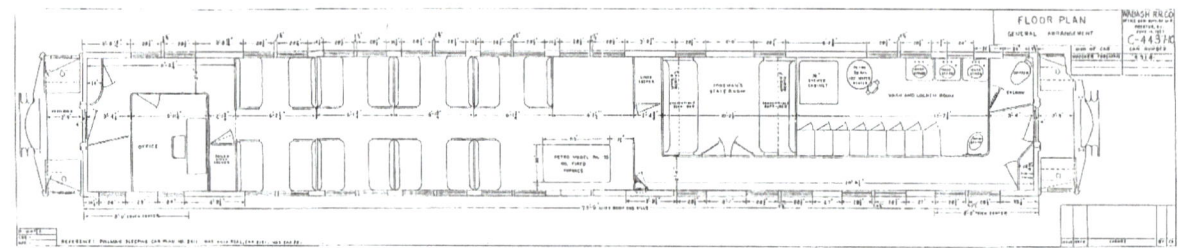

Wabash Plan for 4318

Under Norfolk and Western ownership, the car was repainted four times in varying shades of MoW light and medium green and lastly black with a silver roof. N&W's successor, the Norfolk Southern Railway, kept the car painted black and applied company letter board and NS 564318 was applied to each side. In 1984 it received a fresh coat of paint inside and out for an employee excursion special: The interior was painted gloss white and the outside was lettered "Santa Claus Express." It retained that lettering until it was sold in 1995.

564318 resided in several different locations about the NS system. In 1991 it was in Decatur, Alabama and in 1992 it was in Decatur, Illinois. The last Foreman to ride the car recalls that the car was seldom used and that the two external 120-gallon water tanks were moved to the ceiling of the men's room to prevent freezing in the Illinois winters.

The car ended service in 1994 and was included in the auction in Birmingham, Alabama at which Norfolk Southern disposed of its entire steam passenger excursion fleet. Only one other car in the Villa series, Villa Falls, survives at the Illinois Railway Museum, but its restoration is unlikely due to its current state of decay.

564318 in Norfolk & Western Maintenance of Way Service in June 1983

The Acquisition

In the spring of 1995, Norfolk Southern announced that they were ceasing passenger excursion operations, and that all related equipment would be sold at auction in Birmingham Alabama. They also scraped together all the other old equipment and parts that were no longer useful and added that to the sales sheet. The Villa Real was included in the sale.

I was returning to Huntsville from a business trip to Arizona when my flight was diverted to Birmingham because of bad weather at my connection location in Dallas. That gave me a golden opportunity to inspect and photograph the car. It appeared to be in pretty good shape. When I got back to Huntsville, I called Herman and asked him if he would like to go together and buy a Pullman. He said "Why not."

Villa Real at the Birmingham auction

The auction structure required that a letter of credit (LOC) be presented to the auction company ahead of time. That LOC verified your established bid limit. I guessed at the sales price for the car and added 25% to determine the LOC amount that I setup through my bank.

The auction became a bidding frenzy with items selling for much more than expected. When the time came for the Villa Real, the price went through my bid limit on the third bid. I was disappointed and told Herman that we did not get the car.

At that time, I was the President of the North Alabama Railroad Museum in Huntsville. I was working with John Baker, the Norfolk Southern Vice-President of Public Relations, to get NS to donate two miles of track from an abandoned line. I was talking to John shortly after the auction and found out that he had purchased the car. I asked, "John, what are you going to do with that car?" He said, "I don't know, I just bought it on a lark. I thought I might be able to convert it to a business car." I said, "Well, I was bidding against you." He responded, "If I had known that, I wouldn't have bid." I told him "Well, if you ever want to sell it, call me up and make me a deal." Two weeks later, he called me up and offered me the car for what he paid for it. I said, "GREAT! Where do you want the check sent?" So, Herman and I came to own the Villa Real.

The auction sale came with a free move anywhere on the NS system. The North Alabama Railroad Museum owned a siding in downtown Huntsville and the car was moved to that location on the Friday of Memorial Day weekend in 1995. Unfortunately, I was out of town when it arrived.

My office was adjacent to the track leading to the NS intermodal terminal in Madison Alabama. Some of the people who worked for me witnessed the car arriving as the train to Huntsville worked the intermodal terminal with the Villa Real on the rear.

Villa Real on the siding in downtown Huntsville

Villa Real Restoration Summary

The restoration of the car turned out to be a daunting task and much more demanding than first anticipated. One of my favorite sayings was very applicable: "Kill one problem and five of its friends show up at the funeral." The order of things to be restored was dictated by the survivability of the car, the availability of parts and materials, and what tasks were most desirable to work on, with survivability being the top priority. So, most of the areas of restoration did not have a continuous flow from start to finish. There were often several different projects overlapping each other. For the first twenty-two years, all of the work on the car was done during one weekend day per week. Work on some of the parts that were stored at our house could be done during the week. Weather also played a part in what was being worked: exterior work was done in good weather and interior work was done in poorer weather.

The first order of business was to secure the car from leaks and vandals. All of the MoW interior and roof appurtenances were removed, and the holes repaired. Quarter-inch thick polycarbonate was added to the exterior sash rails of the windows openings to seal the car. The next step was to start the exterior restoration with complete removal of the old paint. In order to document the layers of paint, sanders and wire wheels were used rather than sand blasting. There was also an extensive amount of "Pullman Disease," where the lower part of the body sides rust out from the inside. It took most of two years to cut out the bad side steel, clean and prime the remaining steel, and weld in new plate steel and sill frames along the sides.

A lot of time was spent gathering the missing parts. Many parts were obtained from the scrapping of Clover Lodge at the B&O Railroad Museum in 1996. Nearly all of the parts to restore the section areas, as well as the restrooms, Bedroom A and Bedroom B came from that car. Some were obtained when Villa Roads was scrapped in Norfolk, Nebraska. Illinois Transit Assembly in St. Louis and the Illinois Railway Museum near Chicago were also great sources for parts.

The trucks were upgraded to Hyatt roller bearings the summer of 2000 so that the car could continue to be moved by rail. The original friction bearings were a limitation when the car was moved to Raleigh in early 1998. The Hyatt roller bearings and wheels came from a scrapped car in West Virginia.

eBay was also a great source of missing parts. When Herman and I acquired the Villa, there were only twenty-four of the original 86 light fixtures and three of the original eight sinks present. None of the five toilets and all of the decorative brass shelving were gone. The invention of 3-D printing in the past few years was also a great benefit for acquiring parts that are "non-collectible," such as seat end brackets, Garland vent covers, etc. Over the twenty-six and one-half years that the car was under restoration, we managed to reacquire or make all of the missing hardware for the car.

We also found that the sidewalls were not the only exterior steel with Pullman Disease. The rounded lower edge of the clerestory roof had also developed pin holes through the paint that would allow water into the car. A process was created to cut out the old steel, restore the exposed steel wall/roof support interface, remove and replace insulation, bend and shape new steel and weld it back in place. Over 90 feet of roof steel edge was replaced. All of the steel window frames were also found to require attention to each of the lower corners. The corners had to be cut out, cleaned, and appropriate new steel formed, fitted, and applied and then welded back together.

A goodly number of years were spent removing old paint from the interior of the car. There were thirteen coats of paint on the walls at the thickest places. We did cross-section analysis of some of the paint chips to determine the colors used on the car at the different stages of operation. We also tested the paint and found that the bottom four layers were lead based, which required special handling for disposal. We swept the paint chips and dust into five gallon buckets and turned them in as hazardous waste.

The restoration was completed in early 2021. Rather than presenting a detailed chronological history of the restoration, I have covered the restoration by car area or by item.

Exterior Wall Steel

Initially the Villa's exterior seemed to be in pretty good shape. But, it turned out all the surface plates that were screwed on to the sides were covering up rusted areas. That was when I learned about something I call "Pullman Disease". The rust was not from the outside, but from the inside out, and more extensive than I had thought.

The area around the windows was not completely sealed by design. Water could penetrate around the steel interfaces and get down inside the wall sections. The walls were filled with horsehair felt insulation that sagged down over the years. Dust and dirt could also penetrate the same cracks. The result was a large horsehair sponge where water and dirt created mud in the bottom of the walls, and it rusted from the inside out.

Example of the rusted holes behind the screwed on cover plates.

The damage on both sides of the car was fairly extensive. In some places, the lower structural support steel was also destroyed and needed to be replaced. The first section I repaired using one long piece of steel. I found it was difficult to hold in place and the length of the weld had to be managed to prevent heat warping. After that, I worked in lengths of two to three feet at a time. The steel is 10 gauge, which is almost 3/16-inch thick.

New structural support steel added to the outside.

I made the mistake of predrilling and tapping the rivet holes in my first piece of replacement steel, which made it almost impossible to correctly align and install the "rivets." On subsequent repairs, I drilled and tapped the holes afterward. I also discovered that a 3/8-inch round head slotted screw is the correct size to replace a rivet. The slot in the head was concealed with epoxy and filler.

New side steel welded in place.

While on a business trip to San Diego, I visited an old ferryboat museum and got into a conversation with a Navy chief who was doing restoration work. I learned about West Systems Marine Epoxy and fillers that became the staple supply for doing surface repairs to the steel and hiding imperfections in my welds. I also used it to fill the slots in the round head screws so that they looked like rivets.

More examples of the extensive steel damage.

Unrepaired area next to a repaired area.

I became very proficient at cutting a straight line using an angle grinder with a cut off wheel. I was able to accomplish most of the steel replacement within the first two years before moving to Raleigh. Little did I know that there was a lot more steel work yet to be done.

The steel repair on both sides is complete and covered with red oxide primer

Exterior Paint History

When we were removing the exterior paint, we found the remaining lettering from various parts of the car's MoW history. The car had been stripped and repainted by the Wabash Railroad when they took possession of it from Pullman. The car was painted Tuscan red with white letters that said "WABASH." The car number was 4318 and there were Wabash "Flag" emblems over each truck. When Wabash converted the car to MoW in 1957, they repainted the car silver and changed the lettering to red.

Both red and white Wabash lettering Exposed

The "Flag" emblem on the car side

When Wabash merged with Norfolk and Western, the car received another round of paint. (Actually, it was painted several times while in NW MoW service.) The car was also renumbered 564318.

Norfolk and Western lettering and numbering. If you look closely, you can also see the red Wabash 4318 numbers in the center.

N&W MOW herald adjacent to one of the windows

Clover Lodge

In 1996, Herman and I had visited Illinois Transit Assembly in St. Louis to scrounge and buy Pullman parts for the restoration. They had passed my contact information to the B&O Railroad Museum that was trying to dispose of a Pullman car. The curator of the museum called me and said they had a car that they were scrapping, and it might have some parts I was looking for. This was on a Tuesday, and I asked, "when are you going to scrap the car?" and he said, "Next Monday". I swallowed hard and made arrangements to meet him at noon at the museum on Friday. Without having seen the car, I loaded my tools, generator and hooked my small 8-foot long trailer to my Taurus station wagon and drove from Huntsville to Baltimore.

I arrived at the B&O Museum on Friday at noon. I found out that the car was not at the Museum but stored in a shipyard. We drove out to the shipyard to inspect the car. The car was Clover Lodge, an upgraded 10-5 heavyweight sleeper.

Clover Lodge stored in a Baltimore shipyard

The car was an absolute wreck. There were no windows left in it and the inside was a mess. However, I could see beyond the mess and the car was a goldmine for the parts that were needed to complete the Villa Real.

The curator initially wanted to negotiate for some of the individual parts, but I offered him a fat sum to salvage anything that I could from the car. He was agreeable and I wrote the B&O Museum a check. Before he departed he said, "You need to be aware that homeless people and gang members sleep in this car at night. When you come down in the morning, just pound on the car side with a hammer and then wait in your Taurus for a few minutes." The next morning, I did as he suggested and after a few minutes three people climbed out of the car and started walking up the tracks. After a cautious inspection, I determined that I did have the car to myself.

Men's room couch and mirror frame location.

Section area

Bedroom with Hopper

I worked on the car from Friday afternoon through Saturday evening. I pulled out three upper berths, section seats, wall panels, trim molding, hopper frames and toilets, and various other hardware that would be useful.

At the end of Saturday, I had not gotten everything I wanted. But, the trailer was full, and it was time to head home since I had to be back at work on Monday. I had loaded about 3000 pounds of stuff onto my trailer and the poor Taurus was having a difficult time going down through the Appalachians, making 85 mph on the down hills and 40 mph on the up hills.

The following Monday morning I called the Curator of the B&O Museum and asked if he would hold off the torch so I could repeat the process the next week. He agreed and I repeated the process and drove to Baltimore again on Thursday. I arrived in Baltimore around lunchtime on Friday and immediately went to work on the car.

There were two memorable and humorous events that occurred on this second trip.

The weather on Friday was drizzly with a warm front arriving in the afternoon. I had hauled several items to the trailer and was already damp from the drizzle. The weather front was proceeded by a thunderstorm with a lot of wind. Since there were no windows, the wind whipped through the car with a frenzy. The wind caught an old feather pillow with a torn case and filled the section area where I was working with blowing feathers. It only lasted for a few minutes, but when I looked at my clothes, I was completely covered in feathers where that had stuck to my damp clothes. I did not think to get a picture.

The second memorable event was on the trip home. I was driving south on I-95 between Baltimore and Washington DC when I ended up in traffic directly behind the Hershey's Kissmobile. This was a Hershey spin-off of the Oscar Meyer Weinermobile. It looked like four very large Hershey's Kiss candies stuck together, each complete with the tassel on top, and mounted on four tires.

Buffer Plates and Curtains

The buffer plates on the Villa Real had been removed after conversion to MoW service. Right after we acquired the car, I was told that there were two old Pullman cars at the U.S. Space and Rocket Center in Huntsville. After some driving and searching, I found them back near the Aviation Challenge area at the back of their property. The two Pullman cars had been converted, as a pair, into a B-52 simulator for the US Air Force in the 1950's. Each of the cars had one remaining buffer plate. That presented a challenge because the Space & Rocket Center is an Alabama state government entity.

I made multiple inquiries over the next year about salvaging those buffer plates. The entrance to each of the cars was accessed using wooden steps fastened to the buffer plates. The flexible movement of the buffer plates made the steps unstable. I met with the curator to discuss the situation and proposed a solution. I would remove the steps and the buffer plates and clean and repaint the ends of the cars. Then I would rebuild the steps and fasten them to the cars more securely to eliminate the safety hazard.

B-52 Simulator (ex-Pullman Car)

He agreed to scrap the buffer plates to the North Alabama Railroad Museum unconditionally. NARM is on the recipients' list with the state property disposal office. Since the transfer was unconditional, NARM could then dispose of them to the Villa Real project.

I quickly realized that my tools were nowhere near large enough. That led to the purchase of a 1-inch socket set, a 4-foot long pipe wrench and a 24-inch Crescent wrench. I built a 12-foot beam out of 2 x 6's that would sit on top of the car roof and would be held in place with ratchet straps clipped to the rain drip edge of the roof. I used a come-a-long from the beam to raise and lower the buffer plates.

Beam and come-along used to raise the buffer plates onto the Villa Real

The original buffer plates on the Villa Real did not have the vertical support rods on either side. Those are necessary to prevent the buffer plate from sagging too close to the coupler. The brackets that support those rods at the top of a car were originally mounted using 1-inch diameter hot rivets. It was challenging to drill the holes to mount those brackets. The steel in that area is 2-inches thick because of the crash beams in the end of the car. The holes were step-drilled starting at 1/8 inch and working up to the 1inch diameter. I was only able to drill 4 holes in a day.

The buffer plate installation was completed just before receiving a job offer from IBM and moving to Raleigh.

The original buffer plate curtains were rubberized canvas. The salvaged buffer plates had curtains, but they were stiff and dry-rotted. They were sufficient to use as patterns, but new material was needed. I found rolls of 12-inch-wide agricultural conveyor belt material at a local farm supply. It was black UV-resistant rubber with a canvas core. It was perfect. Parts were cut from the conveyor belt material and fastened together to form new buffer curtains.

The buffer plate with new curtains installed

Move from Huntsville to Raleigh

In August of 1997, I received a call from IBM asking me to go to work for them in Raleigh. I said, "I can, but I have a big problem. If I can't move my railcar, I'm not coming". After some negotiating back and forth, IBM arranged for a moving package that included moving the Villa Real. I later learned from one of the human resources people that this was the only railcar that IBM had ever paid to move.

I had gotten a quote from NS to move the car and estimated the other costs and IBM cut me a check for that amount. Next came the task readying the car for the move. That included taking all of the hardware that I had acquired that was stored at my house and putting it in the Pullman for transport. Then came the car preparation. Shorty's Truck & Railroad Car Parts in Alexandria, Alabama, was certified to do railcar brake service, so I drove down and swapped valves. The car had ABD freight valves put on for MoW service and they were readily available. After installing the valves and hoses, I arranged with NS for the car inspection. The car had friction bearing trucks and the NS inspector was very leery of accepting the car for shipment with friction bearings. The car had been shopped by NS in Roanoke before shipping down to Birmingham for the auction so the bearings were still pristine. NS was still skeptical, and two more inspectors came out before they agreed that it would be acceptable.

I started working for IBM in early December 1997, but the Villa did not move until January 1998. The car arrived on Martin Luther King Day in 1998. It traveled mostly on local freights, and took eight days to make the 600-mile trip.

Train into Raleigh arriving with the Villa Real

One of my tasks after I arrived in Raleigh was to arrange for a place to park the car once it was delivered. I found a location on a siding next to the CSX yard office in downtown Raleigh.

Villa Real parked on the siding next to the CSX yard office

Electricity

When the car arrived at the siding in Huntsville, there was no electricity available. So, I purchased a generator that had sufficient output to power tools or a welder. When I went down to work on the car, I would load the generator along with the tools into the back of my Taurus station wagon. I would unload it onto a hand truck at the Villa Real site, use it, and then reload it at the end of the day. The problem was the weight. With a full tank of gas, the generator weighed 192 lbs. It took a lot to lift it four times per trip.

Unloading the tools and generator

The generator worked well and was used after we moved to Raleigh. The Villa Real was parked at the CSX yard office in Raleigh next to a baggage car owned by John McFadden. John had a temporary power pole installed next to his car and I started working on getting the same.

I called the electric utility company and asked about getting service. "No problem. All you need is a street address," they said. If you want to have some fun, call the city planning office and request a street address for a railroad car. After months of persistence, I did get someone in the planning office to agree to visit the location and see what I was requesting. They came out and agreed that I could get an address. I then had an electrical contractor install a temporary pole, meter, and electrical box. Once that was in place, I went back to the power company and arranged for service to be installed.

I had acquired a pair of railroad lineside electrical boxes with 100-amp 3-phase breakers. Those would be perfect to get power to the car. One was mounted to the temporary pole and the other was mounted to the underside of the car where there had been a large conduit connection.

The temporary electric pole and meter

The lineside power box installed on the temporary pole

Inside the Car

The original wiring inside the car had been cut off flush at the openings in the walls. That wiring consisted of dried, rotted cloth jacketing over stranded wires. For MoW service, conduit was fastened to the surface of the walls and ceiling and plumbed through the car. All of that conduit was removed early in the restoration. Putting new wires in the original wire chases proved to be a challenge: wiring was run behind metal trim molding and inside wall cavities with no conduits. After some searching in access areas, I determined that the main wiring for the car actually ran through the top of the clerestory roof and was accessible from panels on the outside of the car. From the clerestory, the wiring branched off to the various switches and light fixtures. The path from the clerestory roof took a sharp right angle turn to follow the curve of the main roof down to the walls. It was not possible to use a conventional fish tape to pull new wiring. The solution was to attach a strong nylon string to the end of the original wiring and pull it through from the other end. Then the nylon string was used to pull new wiring into that location.

The car's original electrical service was 32 volts DC. However, I was installing 110 volts AC into the car.   The original round fuse panel had long since been removed, so I installed a circuit breaker box in the corner cabinet location to replace it. The original large conduit ran from that location out to the roof access so the path for the new wiring was now available.

A map was created for the power distribution to the different rooms and parts of the car, including all eighty-six original light fixture locations. The next challenge was pulling the new wires. That was done by feeding the wires down from the roof access.   I had a large pry bar that I used as a spool shaft, accompanied by a very large magnet and rope to maintain tension on the pry bar, as the wire unspooled.

The pry bar, magnet and spools shown in position to pull wire

The original wire connections were wrapped in rubber sheathing for protection behind the access panels. I bought a large truck tire inner tube to cut into pieces to replace that sheathing. It was wrapped around the wires and held in place with tie wraps.

Exterior Paint – Round 1

After finishing the exterior steel work, I was anxious to get some finish paint onto the car. Herman agreed that we should not scrimp on the paint quality, so we decided to go with Imron. Arthur Dubin had published a book entitled *Pullman Paint and Lettering Guide*, which contained dimensional information for the lettering as well as a paint chip for the standard Pullman green color. I found a source for Imron in Raleigh. It turned out that Pullman green was one of the standard color mixes in their computer system. I estimated that it would take three gallons to paint the car. That stuff was a little pricey at about $300.00 per gallon. Imron is a two-part Urethane paint. So, once a sprayer batch is mixed, you paint till you run out. The interesting thing about Imron is that the paint is moisture cured. It uses the humidity in the air to cure the mixed paint. So, it cures quickly in the South.

Top of the clerestory roof painted light grey

I decided to paint the car from the top down on the car, so the top of the clerestory roof was first. Since you can not see the top of the car from the ground, I decided to paint it light grey to lessen the heat absorption in the summer. I also used an industrial oil-based paint for the roof.

The sides of the roof were next to be painted. These needed to be black to have the classical Pullman look. This paint was also an industrial oil-based paint.

The black roof paint applied

I had consulted with an automotive paint expert about applying the Imron. He recommended that a specialty primer paint be applied first to ensure high surface adhesion of the Imron. The masking of the car required covering of the windows and the roof edge and that took six hours. The painting of the sides took two hours, and the cleanup and masking removal took another hour. It was a very long day.

The specialty coating primer applied to both sides of the car

I also researched how the Pullman lettering was applied. It was actually a reverse process. The gold paint for the lettering was applied first and then the lettering stencil was laid upon top. The Pullman green paint was sprayed over the car and the stenciling removed to expose the gold lettering. The original lettering color was Dulux gold. It turned out that this paint and color were still available.

Researching lettering stencils, I found that the original stencils were provided by Demp-Knock, and they were still in business. They no longer had the dies to cut the Pullman stencils, but they still sold the 1-foot-wide roll of tape from which the stencils were cut. On a couple of railroad museum visits, I was able to get straight-on pictures of each of the letters for "Pullman." Armed with the dimension from the Dubin book, I was able to draw each of the letters to scale on blue line paper. I found an engineering graphics firm that could generate copies of 24-inch by 36-inch drawings and made duplicates to use to make my own stencils.

Gold paint applied to the lettering areas

One-foot wide masking tape over the gold paint was the first part of the lettering process. Each of the photocopies of the lettering was then taped down over the top of the masking tape. A scalpel was then used to cut out the lettering and score the masking tape. Once the letters were cut out, the photocopies and the masking tape outline were removed.

The painting of each side took two days. The first day was spent getting the lettering applied and the next day the Imron paint went on. Like the specialty primer, this operation also took nine hours per side to complete. The hardest part of the painting process was finding two consecutive days with good sunshine and little or no wind. Fall offers some of the best weather and I was able to paint both sides on two consecutive weekends.

The homemade lettering stencil over gold paint

The finished Imron Paint

Wheel and Bearing Swap

After the car was moved to Raleigh, Herman and I decided that we needed to upgrade the bearings on the car to roller bearings before the car would be able to move again. I placed a 'wanted to acquire' ad on an internet site for railroad classified ads and received three responses. One was for equipment that was being sold from a defunct railroad museum near Morgantown, West Virginia; one was for a car in North Bay, Ontario, Canada; and another was for two cars in South Carolina.

I took off work for a long weekend and drove to Morgantown, West Virginia first, then on up to North Bay. I also stopped in Detroit to buy some parts from Doug Brown, owner of the car in North Bay. Driving from Detroit to North Bay, I crossed over into Canada at a very remote isolated spot. When the Canadian customs agent asked for my purpose in Canada, I told her that I was going to look at railroad car wheels. She looked at me for a while and then said, "I have time." So, I spent the next fifteen minutes explaining to her about the Villa Real and the restoration project. Apparently, they do not get many visitors looking for railroad wheels.

Returning from North Bay, I drove down across Niagara Falls back into the US and down I-95 to South Carolina before heading home. The best solution was the wheels and bearings in West Virginia. We agreed on a price, and I arranged to meet Ohio Valley Railcar personnel in West Virginia. The wheels and bearings were placed on their truck. OVR would disassemble, clean, and perform any replacement of parts or repairs. Then they would reassemble and certify them before shipping them to Raleigh. Each of the wheels and bearing sets weighed 3000 pounds. So, the total load was 18,000 pounds.

Wheels and bearings in West Virginia

When the truck arrived in Raleigh from Pittsburgh with the renovated wheel sets, I had rented a forklift to unload them. I learned how to drive a forklift as I was unloading the wheels. They were set on wooden rails to await installation on the car.

Unloading the wheel sets in Raleigh.

The red strapped blocks prevented the wheels from rolling into the fork lift.

Amtrak has a contract service facility in Raleigh. I hired some of their employees to do the actual swap. I figured that folks who work on passenger cars for a living would be the best people for the job.

To install the refurbished wheel sets under the Villa, the Dymac folks had arranged for a 100-ton crane to be used for the lift. When the day arrived, a 200-ton crane showed up. The crane company said that the price would be the same, but that was a myth. It takes an hour longer each to setup and tear down the 200-ton crane and we had two placements to do. The plan was to place cables under the equalizer bars and lift the Villa with the trucks attached and roll the old wheels out and the new ones in.

The crane company had brought two smaller spreaders but not their large spreader to keep the cables from contacting the side of the car. So, we waited for another two hours while the large spreader was delivered.

The 200-ton crane and spreaders lifting the car

    The first truck was lifted with no issues and the wheels were swapped just as planned. The second truck proved to be a problem. When the car was lifted and the old wheels dropped, the equalizer arms squeezed toward each other slightly and would not align with the new bearing boxes.

Sling Cables lifting the equalizer bars

I solved the problem by grinding a leading-edge chamfer into the bearing box guides and the truck pedestal. This allowed them to interface and spread back apart when the car was lowered.

The wheel swap that should have been a four-to-five-hour job turned into thirteen hours. Everyone was exhausted and glad to be done.

When Ohio Valley Railcar received the West Virginia wheels for refurbishing, they offered to buy the old wheels and bearings from the Villa Real. That was great! It solved my problem of dealing with the old wheels after they were removed. A couple weeks later I got to use my newly acquired forklift skills again, loading the old wheels onto the northbound truck.

When we removed the original wheels and bearings, we found another problem. There is a sacrificial wear block on top of the bearing box that contacts the equalizer arms. My original plan was to transfer the blocks from the old bearing boxes to the new bearing boxes. It turned out that the old bearing boxes did not have removable wear blocks. It was part of the bearing box casting. We decided to assemble the wheels without the wear blocks and deal with it later.

I contacted the people in West Virginia about the original wear blocks. They had ten of the twelve that were needed, which they shipped down to Raleigh. That left me to find two more. We had a friend in Huntsville, Bill, who was a blacksmith. I talked to him to see if he could make me two plates to match the others. He said that he could, so I shipped him one of the cast wear blocks. A few weeks later, he shipped the new wear blocks back to me.

An original sacrificial wear block is in the background and a newly built one is in the foreground

I did not want to repeat the same circus by bringing in a crane to install the wear blocks. I calculated that I only needed to lift each of the equalizer arms by 3 inches in order to insert the wear block. I found some 20-ton bottle jacks that would be able to lift one equalizer arm. I needed two jacks since both equalizer arms had to be lifted for the center bearing box. I used some angle iron and pipe to weld up a bracket that would straddle the equalizer arm and provide an interface for the jack to keep it from sliding off. Sheets of ½-inch-thick steel and oak planking were used to provide a lift base. Over the course of four weeks, all of the wear blocks were installed.

The equalizer arms being lifted to insert the wear blocks

The new wheels and bearings are in place.
The surfaces have been cleaned and red oxide primer applied.

Men's Room Wall and Couch

The wall between the men's room and Bedroom C had been removed, a shower, wall lockers, and a water heater were added as part of the MoW conversion. Two 150 gallon water tanks were suspended from the ceiling.

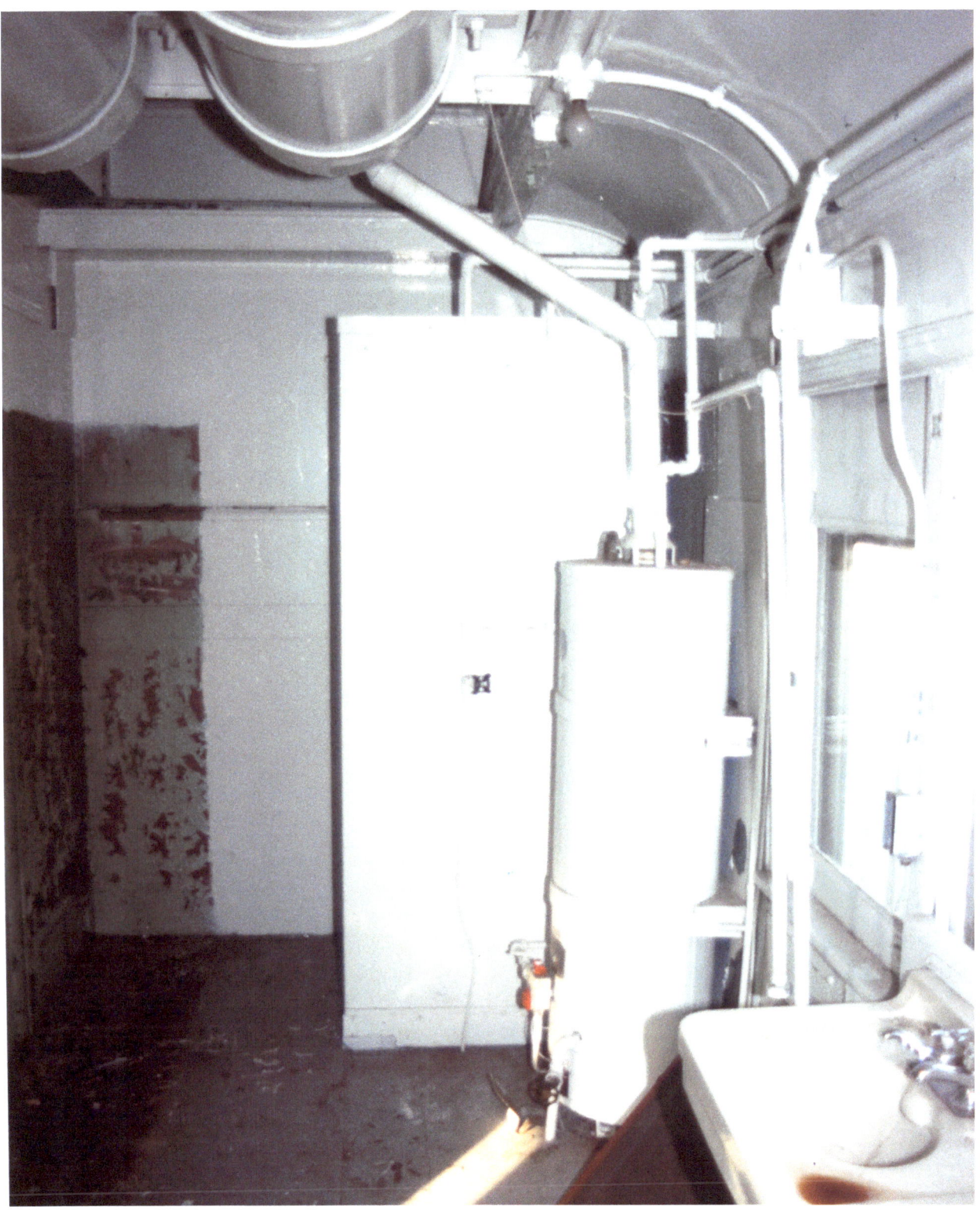

Men's room as received with the lockers removed

The first task was to get all of the MoW "stuff" out of the car. The hot water heater was easy, but the shower proved to be more difficult. The fiberglass shower base was filled with concrete to make it more stable. The use of a sledge hammer made it light enough to cut up and remove. The overhead water tanks required some finesse. I built a 2x4 frame under the tanks so that I could loosen the tanks and patch the roof holes where the bolts had been located. The tanks were then lowered down. The only way to remove them from the room was to push them out one of the windows.

Men's room with "stuff" removed. The shower base with concrete is on the right.

The bedroom door for Bedroom C had been welded over with 16-gauge plate steel. Before the new wall could be built, that door had to be reopened.

Cutting out the welds on Bedroom C door frame.

The new wall was constructed using ¾-inch square steel tubing and 1/8-inch sheet steel. The steel tube was bolted to the car and the flat steel was welded to the steel tube. All of the steel trim molding, mirror frame and couch were obtained from Clover Lodge.

The first piece of new wall steel installed

The wall steel is complete to the ceiling. Trim molding and mirror frame attached

The Clover Lodge couch was test fit before proceeding

Next to the couch was a small settee. I had only seen Pullman photos that showed what they looked like and had not found a real one to measure during any of my railroad museum visits. However, I did have the holes in the men's room wall where it had been mounted as a guide for dimensions.

Someone had dumped a small couch in the CSX dumpster, near where the Villa Real was parked. From its position, I could see the support springs on the underside. I gave it a quick inspection and took some measurements and determined that I could use the springs to make a settee. I salvaged the spring frame from the couch and took it home. I was able to modify the spring frame and build a wooden frame to support it.

New wood settee frame with modified springs attached. Below the wood frame is the steel base that I built to support it inside the car.

I took the completed assembly to B&G Upholstery and Bill was able upholster the seat to match the couch and the Pullman photographs. The back of the settee was nothing more than a wooden frame with padding and upholstery.

The wall is complete and the reupholstered couch has been installed

Men's Room Floor Failure

The concrete floor in the area under the triple sink was found to be heavily fractured and failing due to freezing and thawing of water that had gotten underneath the concrete. I started chipping out the concrete and found that the sink drainpipe that went through the floor had failed. Wastewater had been being dumped under the concrete for years.

The floor consisted of flat steel, then one and one-quarter inches of oak spacers and horsehair felt insulation, followed by more flat steel, and finally covered with two inches of concrete. All of the layers of the floor had failed. After I removed the failed material, you could stand on the track with your head in the car.

The men's room floor under the triple sink

I squared the hole and then added a steel cross-support under the floor, attached to the car frame. I welded in a new steel sleeve for the drainpipe to prevent any further possibility of damage. I added more flat steel and then replaced the oak spacers.

New steel floor plate, added as the first layer, along with oak spacers

I used flat urethane foam insulation rather than the horsehair felt. The final layer of steel was put in place, and it was ready for concrete. Thomas Sayre, a good friend and concrete expert, provided the material to complete the final layer. After the new concrete was poured, the new drainpipe sleeve was cut flush with the floor.

The concrete floor is re-poured, walls painted and the sinks installed

The men's room with the new linoleum floor in place over the location of the hole.

Vestibules and Steps

Sometime during the MoW years, the floor of the vestibules had been removed due to rust damage. In its place was open-grid roof walk salvaged from a freight car. The original floor was flat steel with rubber tile glued to the surface. Over time, the tile dried, cracked, and water got under the tile. That rusted away the steel. I decided that I did not want to put tile down on the platform, so selected steel deck plating with a raised diamond-pattern.

Vestibule platform with the open-grid roof walk removed.

The roof walk was removed, and the platform surface was cleaned and primed. The new deck plate was cut to size. The section of the deck plate that extends over the buffer plates is hinged so that it can flex as the railroad car moves when coupled to another passenger car.

Diamond-pattern deck plate installed in one of the vestibules

The side walls that support the steps were next to be restored. Additional surface steel was added to support each of the steps because the original steel was so rusted.

Step side steel with the additional support steel removed. Condition is typical of all four steps

The original structural steel was evaluated and replaced as necessary. One corner had also been hit and caved in on the corner post. The structural steel underneath was also damaged.

The side steel has been cut open to clean out and assess rust damage. Primer was applied to preserve the bare steel.

New support steel for the step and corner have been added

The support steel also provides the attachment point for the trap mounting bracket. The new support steel is ¼-inch-thick plate that is both screwed and welded into place.

Wall steel was cut back and new surface steel was welded into place. Three-eights-inch round head screws were used where the rivets had been located

The last part of restoring this area was replacing the corner post damage. A piece of 1/8-inch plate was cut to size and then folded in a metal brake to create the step next to the wall. The radiused portion was formed with a very large hammer and blocks of wood.

The new corner has been screwed into place but not yet welded

The new corner has been welded into place and coated with primer

Only one of the steps required significant work. This bottom step had been replaced with a piece of diamond-pattern deck plate. The attachment point had major rust damage and was not structurally sound. The vertical wall on the truck side had been replaced with a piece of ¼-inch flat steel before the car was received.

The step that required the most work

Bottom of step showing extensive rust damage

The rusted area has been cut out. The bottom step has been removed and the ¼-inch side plate was curved to match the original profile.

New plate steel is welded into place and the weld ground smooth

The original side plate has a rolled round edge and it flares out at the bottom step. The ¼-inch flat plate had neither. I was able to add the flare at the bottom by bracing a 4 x 4 block of wood between the flat plate and the truck frame and fiercely beating the outside edge of the flat plate with a sledge hammer. I gave it my best Babe Ruth swings. I used a piece of ½-inch round steel rod that was contoured to the edge and welded in place to replicate the rolled round edge.

I bought a replacement bottom step from the Illinois Railway Museum on one of my parts scrounging trips.

The repair work is complete, the bottom step is installed, and new paint has been applied

Dutch Doors and Traps

The Dutch doors on the vestibules had been removed sometime during MoW service. Finding replacements proved to be a challenge. I found one pair of upper doors in storage at the North Alabama Railroad Museum. After many inquiries, I learned that they had come from a car that had been scrapped but were not earmarked for any particular purpose. The Museum board voted to pass those along to the Villa Real project. A complete pair of doors also came from Ed Jocelyn. He was reworking his car to replace a vestibule with an open platform and no longer needed those upper doors, so he sold them to me. The other pair of lower doors came from the B&O Railroad Museum. They had been sitting outdoors leaning up against a tree and were sunk about six inches into the mud.

The restoration of the upper doors was fairly straight forward, mostly just removing paint, fixing any rust damage, and squaring the window openings where they had been modernized. The hinge mounting points were unsuitable and I ended up welding up the original threaded holes and drilling and tapping new ones.

The lower doors required extensive work. The rust damage required replacement steel in places, especially the area sunk into the mud. The bottom few inches were completely missing!

Example of the lower door damage

The first step in the restoration of the lower doors was to clean up and cut away the bad steel. That made the doors several inches too short. Fortunately, the interior dimension was 1 inch so square steel tubing could be used to rebuild a frame structure for the doors. Two of the doors were unique with open backs. I decided that these needed to be covered over to match the other doors.

The new steel tubing in place on the door bottom (open back shown)

The surface steel was then welded into place and a surface coating of West Systems epoxy was used to cover any weld imperfections.

The surface steel in place with partial welding completed.

The bottom sheet steel has been welded into place

The surface epoxy applied followed by a coat of red oxide primer

Two coats of primer paint were applied prior to installing the doors on the car. Before the final Imron paint was applied, a specialty primer was used to enhance the adhesion of the urethane paint.

The finished door restoration.

The Trap Doors

The trap doors were also missing from the car. Like the vestibule floor, they were covered with rubber tile and had long since rusted away. I did not want to put carbon steel traps back on the car. I obtained two pair of trap doors from Illinois Transit Assembly that were from more modern stainless steel cars.   These were slightly bigger than the original traps and there were no brackets for opening or closing.

The original opening and closing mechanisms for the Villa Real were intact, but the connection to the actual trap had been cut off. I fashioned new shafts to replace those on the original mechanism but needed to have a way to connect to the trap itself. I decided to use some three-quarter-inch socket-set shaft extensions. They were made from hardened steel and could be used to interface to the square end that I ground onto the built shafts. I contracted with a machine shop to make brackets that would hold the shaft extension to the trap. The other end of the trap would rotate in a bracket that fastened to the wall of the car body. I cut down the traps down to fit the Villa Real openings. The surfaces were cleaned, and primer applied before assembly.

One of the traps with all of the brackets and shafts in place and primed

Section Area

Only seven of the ten sections were intact when we received the Villa. The other three had been removed to make room for the oil-fired furnace (later replaced with a propane-fired furnace) when the car was converted to MoW. The vertical center beam of the window next to the furnace had been removed and steel welded over the window openings. The clerestory ceiling next to the furnace had a 14-inch diameter hole cut through for the vent pipe.

Section area where the furnace had been located

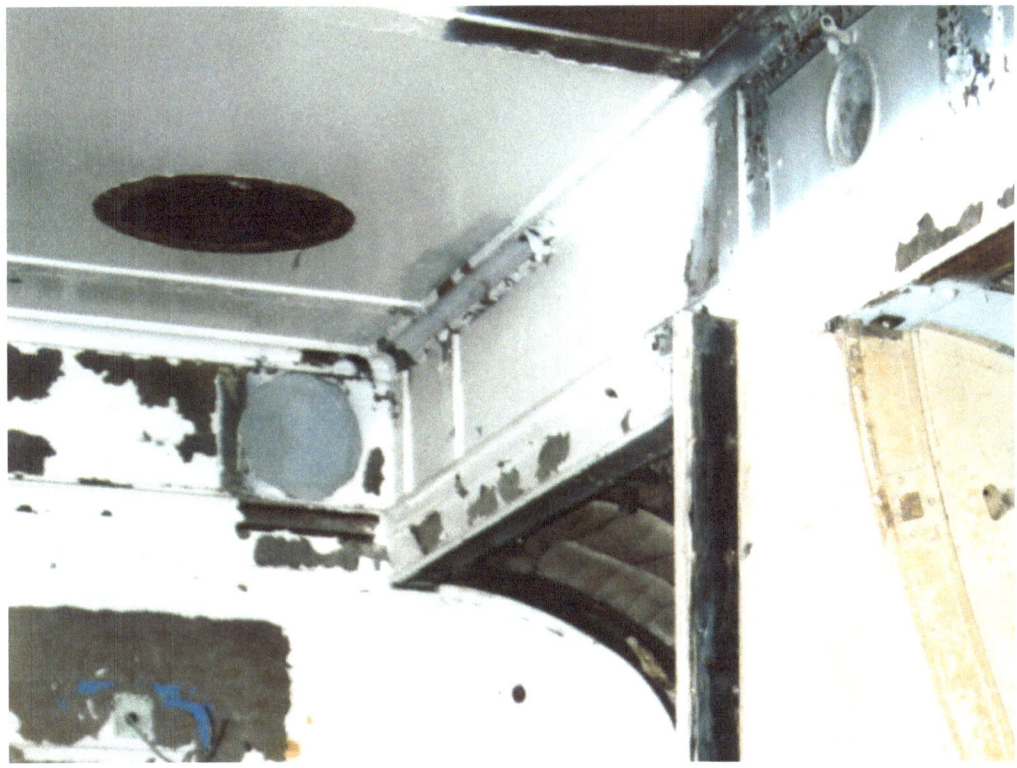
Ceiling with vent pipe hole

The heater ducting was suspended from the ceiling and cut through the walls into the bedrooms, men's Room and the ladies' Room.   The furnace had been removed when I received the car, but the ducting and vent pipe remained.

The first step of this phase of the restoration was to replace the dividing wall between the two sections. The berth divider wall from Clover Lodge was mounted into position. It required further modifications because it was a three-quarter section wall and the Villa Real had half section walls.

The berth divider wall from Clover Lodge installed

The old horsehair insulation was removed and replaced with fiberglass batting. The seat frames that I salvaged from Clover Lodge were modernized versions with the scroll ends. I traded two of the double-ended seat frames to the Illinois Railway Museum in exchange for the older rounded versions. One of those was mounted to this section wall and brackets attached to secure it to the concrete floor. The wall mounting bracket to support the upper berth had been removed as part of the furnace installation. In the restoration, it was replaced by one from Clover Lodge.

The next step was to replace the curved Masonite panel above the upper berth. The 6-foot long by 4-foot wide panel needed to be curved 90 degrees across the 4-foot dimension. After several frustrating attempts and a couple of broken panels, I made a bracket that would support one edge while I formed the radius and locked in the other edge.

Then it was time to install the new vertical center beam between the windows. It was made using two U channels that were welded together to form the beam.

The plated-over window from the outside

The outside of each window center beam is a piece of steel U channel that provides a structural cover. Several of the other windows had rusted areas that needed either replacement or some level of repair. I had Durham Welding and Brazing form up four of these U channels for the car.

The U channel has been mounted using 3/8-inch round head screws in place of rivets. The screws were fastened into the new center beam.

The first side of the steel plate has been cut out

Both sides of the steel plate have been removed and the new center beam installed. Lexan window protection has also been added.

Upper berth bracket and the Masonite panel installed above the window

Double ended section seat frame

The seat frames that I salvaged from Clover Lodge had modernized scroll ends. I traded the Illinois Railway Museum for the rounded-end version that matched the style in the Villa Real. I stripped and primed the seat frames. The originals had the footings cast into the concrete floor. I welded flat plate to the bottom feet so that they could be bolted to the floor when installed.

I had also salvaged replacement upper berths and hardware from the Clover Lodge. The berths are pretty heavy and mounting them was a challenge. I purchased a drywall lift and modified it to support the upper berths. That allowed me to place them on the lift, crank them up into position and then drop them into the support hinge points on the walls at each end of the berth. Over time, I ended up lifting every upper berth out of its mounts in order to work on the Masonite panels. Eight of the ten Masonite panels had to be replaced, leaving only the remaining two original panels that were salvageable.

The dividing wall has been cut down from three-quarter to half-wall width. The upper berths and section seat frame are installed. Steel has been added to the half wall to provide the same detail as the other sections in the car.

The single seat frames at that end of the section area were a challenge. I had obtained one from Clover Lodge, but it also had the scroll end instead of the round end. IRM did not have one of those to trade. I decided to modify the scroll end to turn it back into a round end. I used some 2-inch poplar to fashion a new round end. Additional steel was welded to the seat frame and the poplar was installed using wood screws. The interface was smoothed using West Systems epoxy.

Single seat frame with added steel and poplar round end

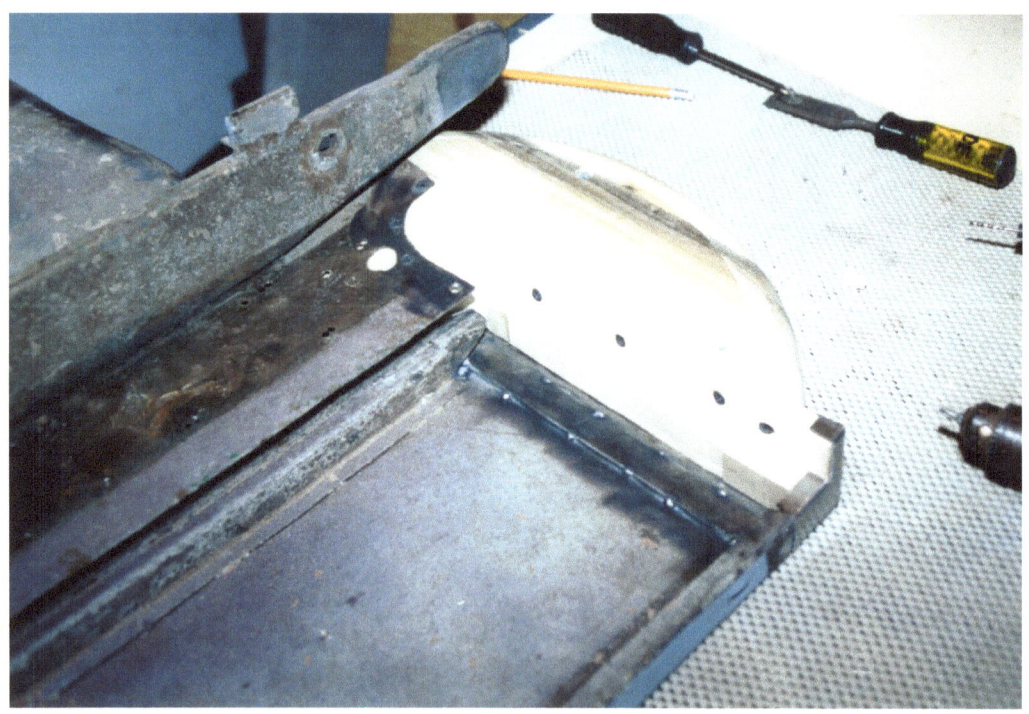

Poplar round end shown from inside the seat frame

The single seat frame on the opposite side presented a different problem: I did not have a frame. I did have half of a double seat frame that was the correct orientation. It had been cut off and a piece of angle iron welded on to provide a second leg support. The wall interface was a 90-degree radius that was fastened into the end wall. I made an adapter for my metal brake that would allow me to bend 16-gauge steel to the correct radius. I removed the old angle iron from the seat frame and welded the formed steel to the edge. Additional structural steel installed and a second piece of smaller-radius steel completed the assembly.

Single seat frame with modified edge shown installed into end wall

Both fabricated section seat ends in place and fastened down

The ducting hole in the wall near the ceiling could not be welded over without damaging the surounding steel trim molding on three sides. I found I could slide a piece of 22-gauge steel in behind that trim molding and the best way to hold the sheet in place was with West Systems epoxy. The trick was to be able to apply sufficient surface pressure to the steel to maintain good contact while the epoxy cured. The solution was to cut a 4 x 4 that could be braced between pieces of clerestory trim steel and use a car scissor jack to apply the pressure.

The duct hole above the end section being patched

The next part of restoration in the corner of this section was to repair the hole in the ceiling. This was a challenge because the back side of the steel in the ceiling had a tar coating that would easily catch fire from the heat of the welder. The hole was large enough to allow using a combination of wire wheel and rags soaked with mineral spirits to clean around the inside of the hole. One problem with welding around a hole this large is warping of the steel. I inserted two pieces of 1/8-inch flat steel above the hole so that it would cover the opening and provide a stable welding surface. I proceeded to weld around the circumference in short bursts that were only about a half inch long.

The ceiling hole welded around its circumference

One of the restored upper berths

Lastly, the wiring and light fixtures were installed and the final finish paint and stain were applied.

The hole in the ceiling is gone and the upper berths are in place

Light Fixtures

There were Eighty-six light fixtures in the car when it was rebuilt as the Villa Real. When we received the car, only twenty-four of the original fixtures remained. All of the section area lower berth fixtures had been removed and the openings welded over with steel. All of the decorative fixtures in the bedrooms, men's room, ladies' room, and hallways were gone. The four vestibule lights and the four aisle light fixtures remained. Just fourteen of the original twenty section upper berth light fixtures, and two of the three bedroom upper berth fixtures remained.

There were two big things that helped with acquiring the needed light fixtures. First, the North Alabama Railroad Museum (where I was president at the time) had a project to have some sand castings made from aluminum for one of its locomotives. I spoke to the company producing those castings about making me some duplicate light fixtures for use in the section area. They agreed. An upper berth bedroom fixture was used as a pattern since were the same as the section lower berth fixtures. I had them cast me twenty-five of those fixtures, which included five spares. Second, eBay launched in 1995. eBay became a great source for parts in the early days. I quickly learned how to successfully bid and acquire parts.

Many of the decorative light fixtures in the restored car were obtained from eBay. I found a couple of the section area overhead fixtures from Illinois Transit Assembly and two more from the Illinois Railway Museum. The hardest fixtures to find were the two chandeliers hanging in the men's and ladies' rooms. I found the first one on eBay; where the owner had sawn it in half and added a chain to make it a swag light. I bought it and was able to remove the chain and restore the light. The other chandelier came from Ed Jocelyn. He eventually allowed me to purchase it.

Most of the light fixtures still had the old cloth covered wiring and were not serviceable. The light sockets themselves were good, but not the wiring. The other issue was the thick layers of paint that had been applied over the years. There was no way to mechanically remove the paint without damaging the fixtures. The light fixtures were brass, so I used full-strength ammonia in a sealed 5-gallon bucket for paint removal. Twenty-four hours in the bucket would strip all the paint and nicely etch the brass surface for refinishing. Brake fluid also works, but it costs more. All paint stripping with ammonia had to be done outdoors because of the fumes.

Pullman painted all of their light fixtures with gold paint. The quality of the brass that they used for casting varied and there would be streaks in the material from different impurities. Also, painted parts do not oxidize or need to be polished to maintain a luster. All of the fixtures received red oxide primer, grey automotive primer, two coats of Ace Hardware Brite Gold paint, and finally two coats of gloss clear lacquer.

All of the light fixtures were rewired using 14 AWG stranded wire. Inserting the wires into the small tubes in the light fixtures was a challenge. The best process involved a small ball of masking tape on the end of a nylon string and blowing the ball through the wire tubes using compressed air. The nylon string was then used to pull the new wires through the fixture.

In the end, I only needed to use eight of the light fixtures I had cast and was able to find all of the other fixtures for the car. All of the light fixtures are outfitted with LED bulbs to reduce the power consumed and increase operating life. Original Steuben globes were found for all of the fixtures, but all of my photos show only cheap hardware store globes. They were substituted to prevent possible damage to the Steuben globes during transit to the Illinois Railway Museum.

Repaired and restored men's room chandelier

One of the cast lower berth fixtures and a section end fixture

Wall light fixtures in the men's room

Hallway overhead fixture

Fans

The car had wall-mounted electric fans in the bedrooms, men's room, ladies' room, and each end of the section area. The section area fans were 12 inches while all of the others were 8 inches. The original fans were manufactured by the Diehl Corporation and operated from the 32-volt DC system on the car.

Very few of the wall fans survived because they were 32 volts DC. There was no market for them. I was only able to acquire one of the original 12 inch fans and it was known to be broken when I bought it. It did provide me with mechanical insight into how the fans operated and were mounted to their brackets.

The Villa Real was not being restored to 32 volts DC but rather 110 volts AC operation. The Diehl Corporation also made desk fans that were similar in size and look, but operated on 110 volts AC. I decided to acquire the 110-volt fans and then modify them to mount into the Pullman wall mount fixtures. The wall mount bracket was cast steel and had a "PULLMAN" nameplate on the front that was made from soft metal and riveted in place. Only three of the fan brackets that I found still had that nameplate.

I was able to find the correct number of 12 inch and 8 inch fans using eBay, over the years, and had the three missing "PULLMAN" nameplates 3D printed in plastic.

Twelve-inch Diehl fan mounted to the end of the section area

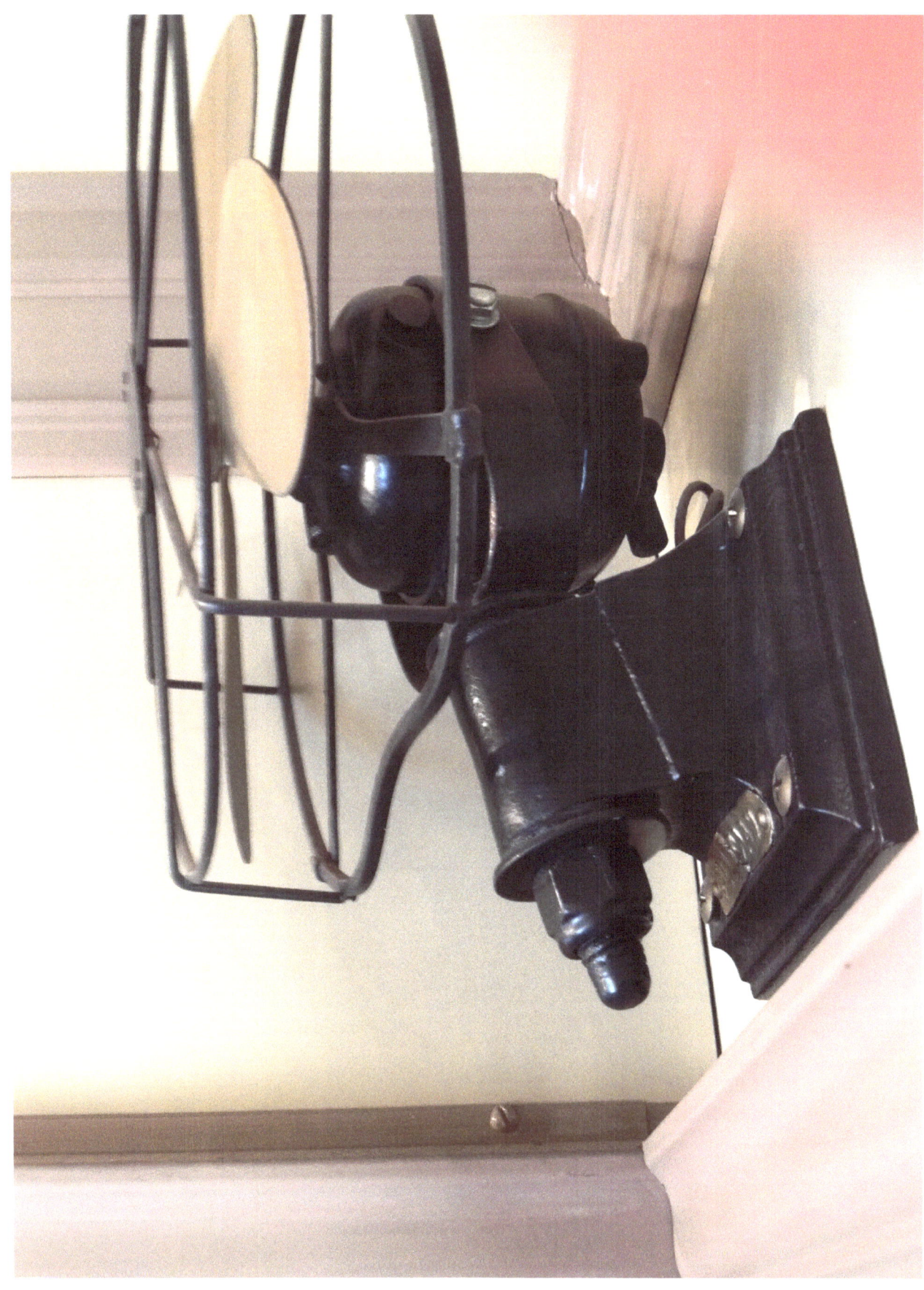

Eight-inch ladies' room fan, wall bracket and the adapter for the Diehl fans

New Upholstery

The Villa Real arrived in Huntsville with only two of the bedroom couches and fourteen sets of section seats. The original upholstery in the car was made of wool and subject to damage from moths, carpet beetles and other insects. None of it was acceptable to use and had been covered over with Naugahyde. That was probably done for the Santa Claus Express excursion in 1983.

After moving to Raleigh, it was time to locate replacement material that looked like it was used on a Pullman car, but be made from a cotton polyester blend that was less susceptible to damage and insects. After some searching, I found a fabric at one of the local upholstery fabric stores and special ordered 100 yards of the material. I did not know how much I would need, but assumed that would be sufficient.

All of the seats and couches were removed from the car and moved to my garage. I built a storage rack in one side of the garage, wrapped the seats and stored them there. B & G Upholstery in Wake Forest, North Carolina was interested in the project and gave us a great rate for doing all the work. In total, he reupholstered all twenty of the section seat sets, two couches for the bedrooms, and the couch and settee for the men's room. It took them a few years to complete everything, doing the work during slow periods in the shop.

The men's room couch had been covered in a dark red leather. We replaced that with a similar dark red vinyl. The before and after pictures of the men's room couch are in the Men's Room Wall and Couch section of this book.

Original fabric pattern

Restored fabric pattern

Interior Paint

The Villa Real interior had a coat of white paint over everything, when the car was received. The car had been used for an employee Christmas train under Norfolk Southern and was sprayed for that event. The paint removal process became an archaeological process to understand what paint colors had been applied in the car at the different stages of its operating life.

As with the exterior paint, I took some of the paint chips from various interior locations within the car to my workplace. I cast the paint chips in resin and then cross-sectioned them to splay out the different layers to show the original colors. I also put the castings in an electron microscope to check at the material composition of the different paint layers.

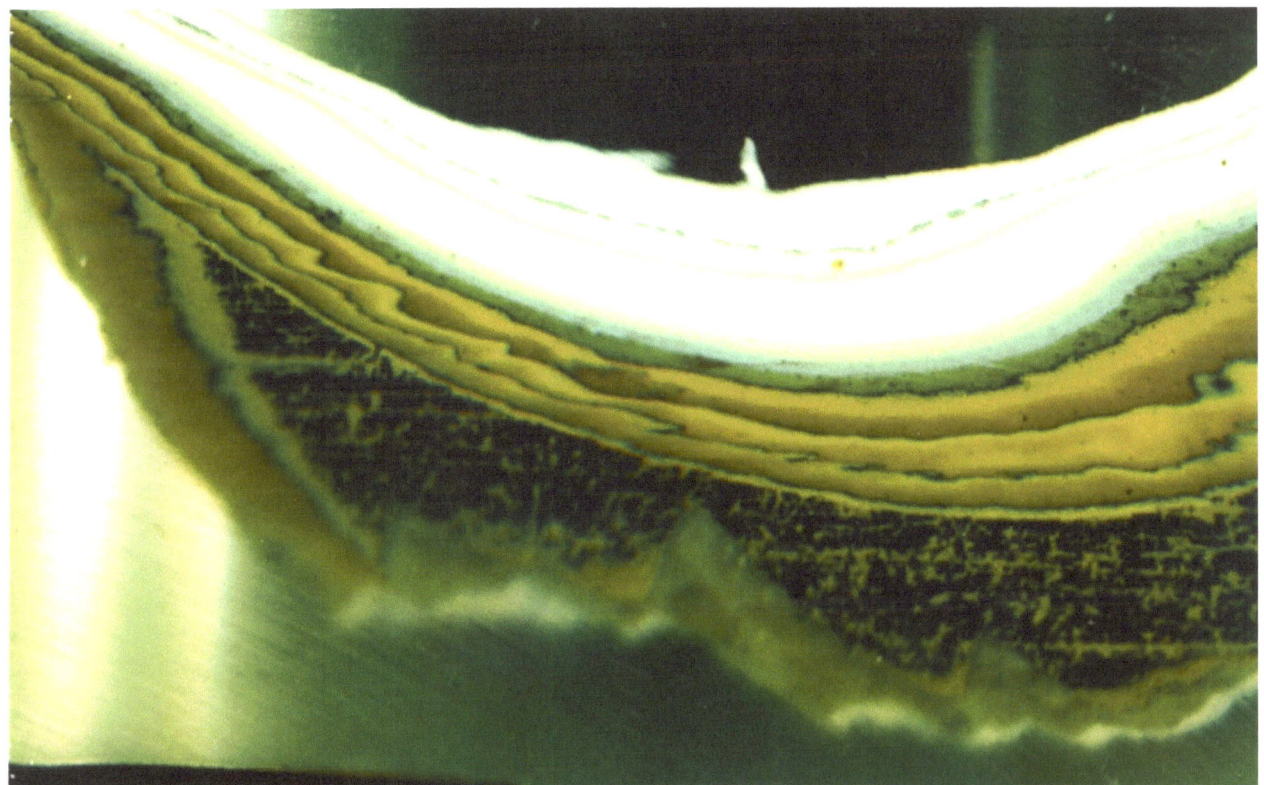

Interior paint cross-section

The final layer of white paint is on the top. Overall, there are thirteen layers of paint. The bottom four were the most interesting. They are the faux wood grain that was originally applied to the car when built in 1911 and probably in 1920 (major upgrade), 1931 (rebuilt to a 10-3), and 1940 (returned from service in Mexico). The biggest problem that I identified was the faux wood grain layers: they contained lead based paint.

The discovery of lead based paint resulted in more safety precautions being taken during removal and required special handling for disposal of the paint chips.

If you want to have some fun, show up at a hazardous waste disposal site with two 5-gallon buckets full of lead based paint chips. Turns out the issue was not the paint. It was the buckets. They were afraid that I wanted to keep the buckets. After I assured them that they could keep the buckets, they accepted the paint chips. That scenario was repeated many times over the years of paint removal.

The long hallway next to the bedrooms and men's room during the paint removal process

Most of the earlier paints were identified as oil-based. The surface steel had not been prepared well, which is why paint adhesion failed over time. After the archaeological work was finished, the bulk of the paint removal was done using a needle scaler and abrasive wire wheels. They did a nice job of removing the old paint and preparing the steel for finish paint.

I found that Rust-Oleum spray primers worked really well, but two coats were required. The first coat was the red oxide rusty metal primer, and the second coat was the light grey automotive primer.

For the final coats, I wanted a highly durable, UV-stable paint. Two part urethane automotive paint was the best solution, but somewhat pricey. The colors were chosen based upon the chip samples that I had removed previously.   There were actually only four colors: beige, light brown, dark red-brown, and almond (ceiling). These paints were applied using an automotive-type spray gun.

The section area showing various states of paint removal and applied primer

I did have some help working on the car from time to time. Herman would come visit a couple of times per year and he was always glad to come work on the car. My wife and daughter would occasionally come down to help remove paint. A couple that lived in a condo nearby was interested in the car and helped for a few weeks. Sometime, homeless persons would stop by the car. If they asked for a handout, I would send them away. If they asked for a job, I would put them to work. If they did a good job, I would invite them back. I had one person who came every week for two years. He did most of the paint removal in the section area by himself.

Herman removing paint from the hallway

The long hallway restoration with new paint applied

The ladies room after restoration showing the colors used

Ladies' Room

The ladies' room was used by the wrecker foreman as an office when in MoW service. The only things remaining from the room's original configuration were the three wall mirrors and the floor tile. There was also some major damage to the center of the floor. Sometime during MoW service, a sledgehammer was taken to the floor, apparently in an attempt to reach the truck pin that would allow the car to be raised off of the truck. (On a Pullman, the truck pin is accessible from under the car.) The floor still had the original rubber tile, but it was covered by many layers of paint. The tiles that had been hammered was damaged, including the concrete floor underneath.

The ladies' room floor damaged concrete has been repaired in conjunction with the men's room floor repair

The duct work from the section area had also been cut through to the ladies room.

Replacement sinks were found at Illinois Transit Assembly and the toilet was found at the Age of Steam Museum in Dallas at the same time the men's room parts were acquired. I decided to wait to remove the paint on the floor until after I had finished the new wall paint. That way I didn't have to worry about masking the floor.

The three large mirrors were intact, but the silvering on the back of the glass was failing. The mirrors needed to be removed from the wall in order to restore the frames, and the old glass was discarded and replaced with new.

The ladies' room ceiling showing where the ducting had been located

The ladies' room floor after the top layer of paint had been removed

The ladies' room has been painted and the new mirror glass installed

Several things were missing from the ladies' room. The corner water cabinet was gone along with the cup dispenser, the vanity shelf, and the two swivel padded chairs. I found the door to the water cabinet, the cup dispenser mechanism, and the "HAIR" bowel for the vanity shelf on eBay.

The water cabinet is similar in design to the one in the long hallway, but slightly smaller. I built it out of mahogany. I knew what the dimensions were because of the gaps in the trim molding and the holes where it had been mounted. The spigot was another item I was able to find on eBay.

The cup dispenser housing was a little more challenging. It was made from folded and welded steel. I had an original dispenser in the long hallway, so I used it as a pattern to make a second one from 16-gauge steel. It was folded and welded to match and the mechanism was installed. The spacing of the mounting holes was transferred from the wall so that it would align with the original holes.

The mahogany vanity shelf was another woodshop project. I had the dimensions from a drawing that I copied from the Illinois Railway Museum. The challenging part was creating the raised lip that extended around the face edge to keep items from rolling off the shelf while traveling. The straight edges were easy, but the curved corner was harder. I built a fixture that would allow me to rotate a disk of the appropriate diameter over the blade on my table saw and create the ornamental groove. I then cut around the contour to create the corner trim.

The corner water cabinet and cup dispenser are shown

I obtained one of the free-standing swivel chairs from eBay and drove to Buffalo, New York to retrieve it. I purchased one chair from the Illinois Railway Museum and was given the broken frame of another chair that had also been exposed to a roof leak. I was able to repair that chair frame so that it could be reupholstered with the others. The wooden bases were sanded and restained then clear urethane was applied. The upper parts were re-upholstered using the same fabric as the section area seats and bedroom couches.

The damaged chair frame after repair and base restoration

Another chair after base restoration

The two restored swivel chairs and the vanity shelf are in place with the "HAIR" bowl

I kept the third restored chair for myself as a reminder of my experience with restoring the car.

Roof Steel

After the Villa was painted the first time, I was still seeing signs of rust stains originating from the roofline and extending down the newly painted car sides. I went to the location that showed the most staining, started removing the roof paint, and found that the edge of the roof just above the rivet line had the same Pullman Disease as the lower sides of the car. In this case, the culprit was not penetrating water but condensation over time that left very tiny holes in the steel above the rivet line. I realized that I would need to rework the entire edge of the roof on both sides of the car.

The roof steel was thinner than the car sides (16 gauge verse 10 gauge). This was going to have to be worked in the same two-foot sections as the steel sides. The other challenge was that this steel had a radius; it was not flat. In addition, since I was still employed at the time, I was only down at the car one day per week. That meant that I had to weld up a hole on the same day that I created it, and I could not be sure what I would find when I cut the roof open.

I picked an area, marked a spot to be opened, and used a cutoff wheel on an angle grinder to cut through the steel. There was horsehair felt insulation behind the cut, so I had to be careful not to set the car on fire. That also applied to the welding. When the roof was open, I removed the insulation (usually damp) to just beyond the cut. A wire wheel and chisel were used to remove any loose rust and metal. Red oxide primer was applied to all the exposed metal surfaces. There was a small trough at the top of the wall where the curved roof section joined to create the drip edge. That trough was what was holding the water. Just before lunch, I would fill that cleaned and primed trough with West Systems epoxy. This much epoxy would take over twenty-four hours to cure, and I did not have that much time for the repairs.

After lunch, I would form a section of roof steel using a radius fixture that I made out of pipe and steel tube. I would "bump press" the steel to create the radius and fit it into the hole several times before declaring it done. The next part was to weld a piece of 1-inch angle iron just behind the edge of the remaining roof steel. That provided a stiffener so that the welded roof panel would not warp and also provided a shield to prevent the 3200-degree Fahrenheit welding splatter from igniting the still liquid epoxy.

As part of the opening process, I ground the original rivets flush rather than drilling them out. The rivets were still pressure welded to the steel frame and provided a surface to drill a new hole for the replacement rivet. Once the new plate was welded in place, I would drill the holes for the rivets. If they were blind, I would drill and tap the steel. If they were through holes, I would use quarter-inch round head screws with nuts and washers to hold the steel in place. The backside of the screw head was buttered with West Systems epoxy with filler; after assembly the slot in the screw was also filled. With the epoxy hardened, a wire wheel was used to clean up the surface of the screw head and primer was applied. All this was done in one day. About seventy feet of roof was worked on each side of the car.

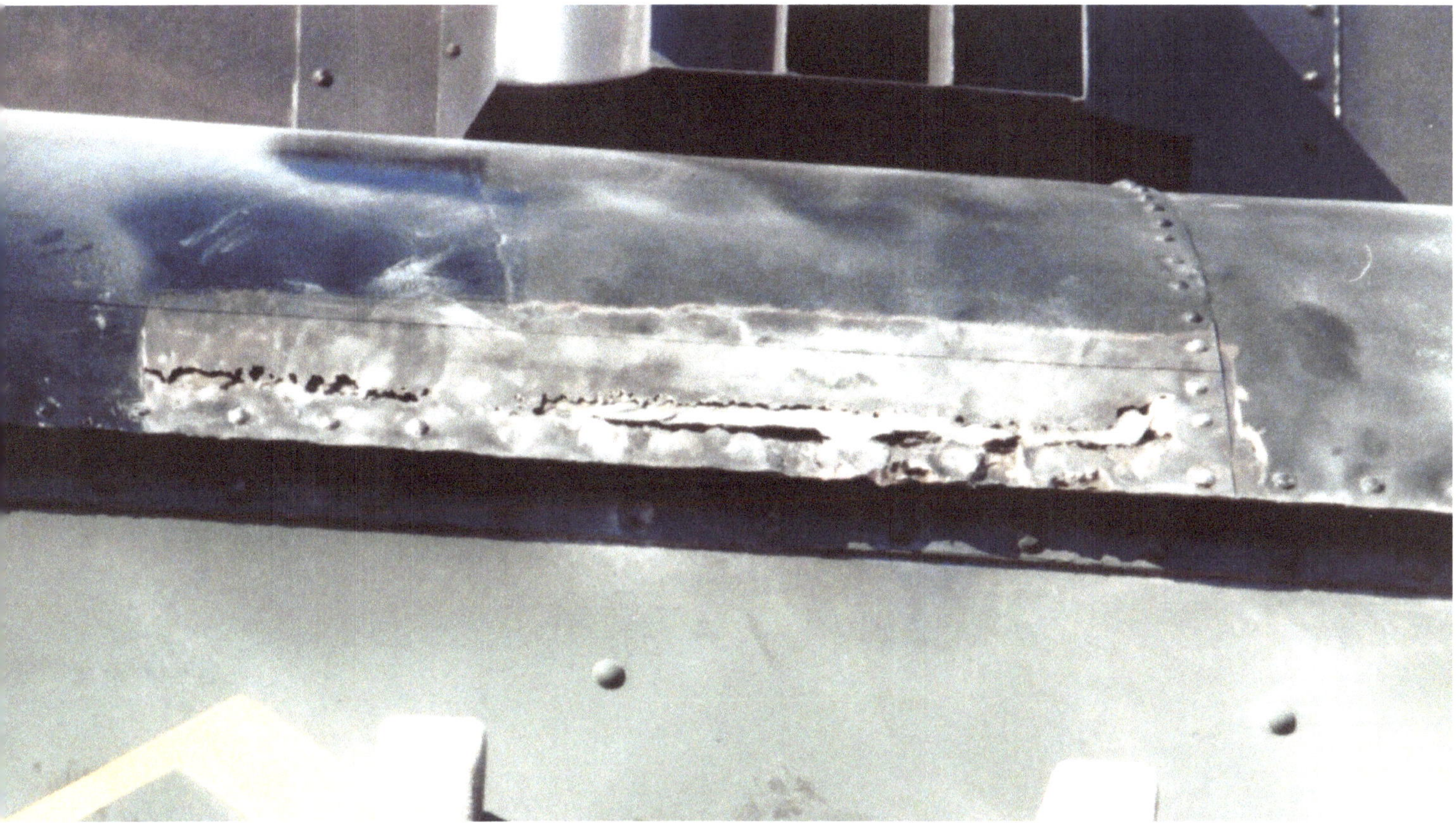

Roof damage exposed

Roof area opened and repaired prior to welding in new steel

Roof area with new steel welded into place before installing rivets and epoxy

This was the most significant area that needed to be opened and repaired because it was leaking around the roof panel seam. The repair took two consecutive days to complete.

New steel welded into place and some of the rivets installed

Window Steel

At the same time that the roof steel was being addressed we found that the steel at the lower corners of every window needed to be worked. Failures occurred around the metal interface that had allowed the moisture penetration into the walls and resulted in the Pullman Disease. Like the roof steel, repairs needed to be accomplished on the same day because the protective Lexan window cover had to be removed to work on the steel and then replaced when the job was done.

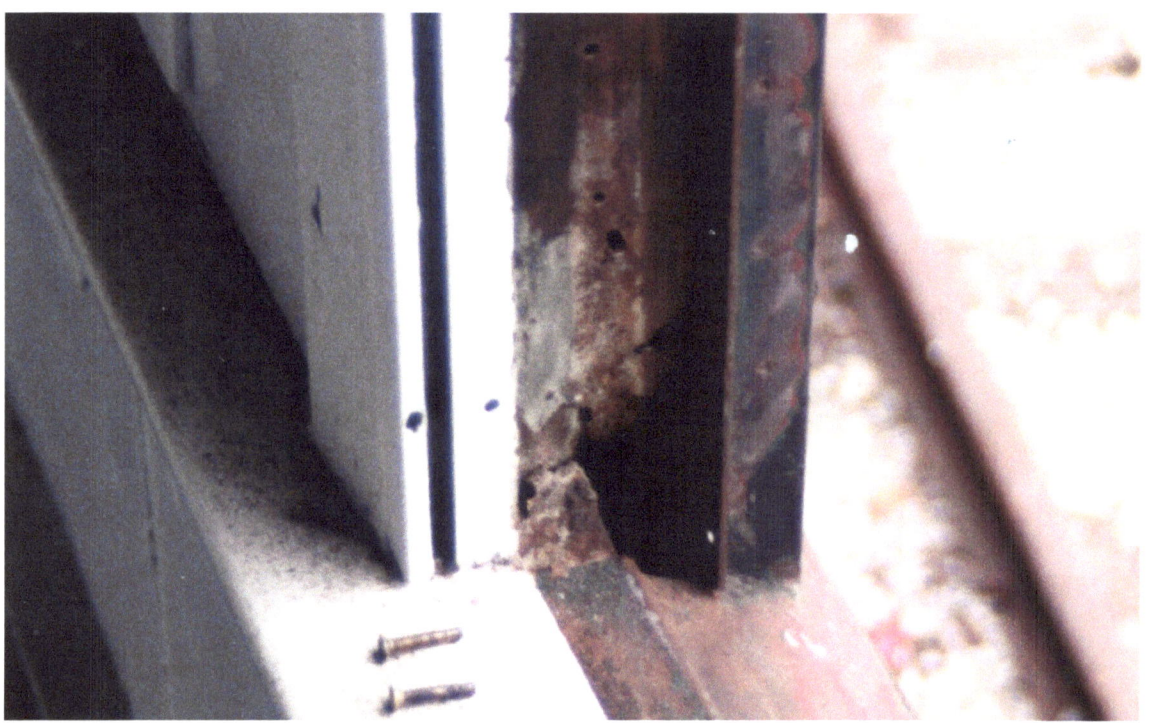

Damage to the side of the window opening. Interior rust also was heaving out the surface around the frame.

The damaged area cut away from another window. The sill has also been removed.

Channel iron has been added to provide support for the window guides and the sill has been replaced. Primer has been applied before adding the remaining steel.

The replacement frame section is on the bottom and the original that is both rusted and heaved is on the top. The rivet is actually raised and is used to hold a smoke deflector from the days of steam engines. The replacement frame was fabricated on site from square tube and flat steel.

The new steel is in place and the West Systems epoxy added

The Lexan has been reattached and a final coat of West Systems epoxy applied. Not bad for one day's work

Steel repair was required everywhere you see red oxide primer

Long Hallway

The long hallway is adjacent to the men's room and the three bedrooms. Some of the details of the long hallway are covered in other sections of the book, so I will not repeat those. There are a few things located in the long hallway that are important enough to mention.

The corner water cabinet was missing when we received the car. I built this one from mahogany using dimensions from those in other Pullman's, the trim openings and the mounting screw locations. This water cabinet is not functional. The latch mechanism and the sink basin were 3D printed.

The tool locker is carryover from the wooden car days and contained tools that could be used in case of a wreck. The saw and axe would be pretty useless in a steel car. When we received the Villa, this locker was painted over and there were no tools inside. The tools were procured on eBay.

Each car came equipped with an ornate hand pump fire extinguisher usually located next to the men's room for the Porter to use. When the Villa Real was rebuilt in 1931, the men's room was moved to the opposite end of the car, but they left the original fire extinguisher in place in addition to the new location. The replacement fire extinguishers were purchased on eBay. This extinguisher has "WABASH" embossed on it and the one near the ladies' room is embossed with "PULLMAN."

The track rack was used for brochures, timetables and other information.
I believe that the area at the bottom held a stack of paper towels.

The cup dispenser was located next to the water cabinet and held small cone-shaped cups

Signage and thermometer at the end of the long hallway

Bedroom Hoppers

The hoppers are are in the double bedrooms: each hopper is a toilet and sink that looks like a chair. If you lift the seat up, it is a toilet. If you fold the seatback down, it is a sink. The bedroom hoppers in the Villa Real had long since been removed when the car was converted to a Tourist car in 1951. Pullman had several different companies making the hoppers for their cars and they were not all the same sizes.

I was able to salvage the toilet, hopper frames and seats from Clover Lodge. Later, I bought some hopper sinks that were the correct size from Ed Jocelyn, who was restoring his own Pullman and converting it to a business car format. One sink spigot mechanism came from Doug Brown, and the other was salvaged out of the Villa Roads in a Nebraska scrap yard.

One of the hopper frames and seats in Clover Lodge

Hopper seat back from Clover Lodge

    I began the restoration by scaping and sanding off all of the old paint. The next step was to put the pieces together to see how they fit and make any repairs. I discovered a major design flaw by Pullman for folding the sink down and up: the hinges on the sink frame were only supported by four wood screws, which supported the cantilevered weight of the sink and water. The brittle side braces were made from cast iron. There were two per sink and I only had one that was not broken. I designed a metal frame from angle iron and square steel tube that would replace the side braces and mount the hinges to it, providing better structure support.

    The height of the hopper frame presented another problem. It was supposed to mount under the wall-mounted mirror frames in the bedrooms. The hopper frames were 1 1/4-inches too tall. I modified the interface to the toilet by removing some wood. The toilet would sit forward by 1 inch, so wood was added to the toilet seat lid assembly and the hopper frame sides. Now, the hopper would fit into the car.

The hopper originally had a small wooden shelf mounted above the frame. I built those from mahogany and fastened them with dowels and glue. I modified brass banister brackets into the front shelf supports. The hopper frame was mounted to the wall first.

The next problem to solve was creating a hole in the floor for the toilet. The concrete floor had been repoured when it was converted to a tourist car and the toilet hole did not exist anymore. There was evidence under the car where the hole had been and there was ribbed steel sheeting now under the concrete. The hole was not round, but oblong to accommodate the bottom flapper valve of the toilet. I built a new hole liner from PVC plumbing parts and flat PVC stock so that there was a cleanout under the car in case of accidental use. It was mostly designed so insects could not get in.

The new hole liner put in place with structural epoxy

The toilets were set in place and bolted to the floor, then the seats were fastened to the hopper frame. The sinks were pinned in place and the spigot assembly mounted.

The toilet surrounds that I obtained from Clover Lodge were incomplete. The Pullman photos I was referencing indicated that there were pseudo chair legs on the corners. There were holes in the surrounds that also showed where they were located, but those legs had been made of steel. I made replacements from oak.

The completed hopper showing the added surround legs, seats and sink in the upright position

Here is the hopper with the sink folded down and the added wooden shelf.

The hopper in the fully closed "seat" position

Bedrooms

For MoW service, the wall between Bedrooms A and B had been removed. The hoppers had been removed when the car was converted to a tourist car. All of the mirrors and shelving were removed. The couches and the upper berths remained.

Bedroom C had been completely removed and the door welded over with steel. It became part of the washroom area with the shower and hot water heater. The upper berth was also removed along with the left side of the bracketing that supported it. After the wall separating Bedroom C from the men's room was restored, it was decided not to restore this bedroom. I had determined a way to eventually add air conditioning to the car by running the ducting down the side of the car where the steam lines had originally been. If the car was to have a permanent home somewhere in the South, it would need air conditioning. Since the final home is the Illinois Railway Museum, the air conditioning is not needed. But parts are not available to do the restoration of Bedroom C.

Bedrooms A & B showing the missing dividing wall and missing hoppers

The connecting door from Clover Lodge did not have any hardware and was covered in about eight layers of paint. I acquired the hardware from a guy in Canada (I cannot remember his name). The connecting door and the pocket door needed to be restored and built into the wall as part of that reassembly.

The pocket door has been stripped to bare wood. Fold down shelves and mirror removed

The restored connecting door with lock hardware installed

The restoration of the bedroom hoppers is covered separately, so not repeated here. Clover Lodge did provide a lot of the parts needed for bedroom restoration. I salvaged the mirror frames above the hoppers, the pocket door, a connecting door with frame, one bedroom door and all the trim molding to go on the missing wall. The shelves and light fixtures came from eBay or from Ed Joselyn.

It wasn't possible to get the pocket door track out of Clover Lodge, so I fabricated a new one by welding together some angle iron and flat steel. The wall frame was made from additional angle iron and channel iron. The floor track for the pocket door and threshold for the connecting door were made from red oak, because it has better wear capability compared to mahogany.

The pocket door is installed. Wall construction and paint are complete

The connecting door is complete and installed adjacent to the pocket door. The pocket door fold-up table has been inlaid with new leather and installed

I only had one bedroom exit door that I salvaged from Clover Lodge. I used the dimensions from that door to make two new doors from 2 inch+ thick mahogany. The lock sets came from eBay, the guy in Canada, and the Illinois Railway Museum.

Bedroom exit doors A and B. A is from Clover Lodge and B was reproduced

3D Printing

One of the best things that helped finish the restoration of the car was the advent of 3D printing. There were several parts that were missing that were not collector's items. Collector's items are things like light fixtures and brass shelves. The non-collector items were usually thrown away when a car was scrapped. Shapeways in New York offers 3D printing in a variety of materials that included several different kinds of plastics and stainless steel. I have 3D CAD software and was able to get dimensions from similar parts or from photographs and mounting-hole dimensions. Here are some of the parts that I had made.

The section divider bracket was the hardest to draw and make it match the original. There are several nylon and stainless-steel parts here. There is a latch block that moves up when the mechanism is turned with a berth key.

Brackets for the vanity shelf in the ladies' room

Soap dispenser for the Men's room sink. I had two but needed a third

Switch plate used in the men's room

Sink fixture used on the long hallway water cabinet

Vinyl Flooring

The men's room, ladies' room and the two hallways had rubber flooring in the Pullman black and green checkerboard pattern. When the car was received, only the ladies' room still contained some of the original rubber flooring. In the other areas the flooring had been replaced by a more modern (1950's) sheet vinyl. Subsequently, it also received several layers of paint.

In 2014 an episode of the PBS show "Ultimate Restorations" covered the restoration of the fish and wildlife car Badger. It was an old heavyweight car that had been used to haul fish and was being refurbished for the Mid-Continent Railway Museum. The linoleum flooring for the car was custom made for the restoration. I contacted the company doing the restoration and found out that the flooring had been provided by Forbo. I then contacted Forbo to see if they would be willing to do a custom linoleum for the Villa Real and received a prompt "No" response. I surmised that they did not have a good experience on the Badger project. However, they did have sheet linoleum that was available in the correct colors.

I calculated the number of 3 inch square tiles that I would need and ordered rolls of the green and black material. Next, I had to figure out how to cut the rolls into the 3 inch squares. I made a fixture from wood and angle iron that allowed me to cut the rolls into 12-inch x 79-inch strips. I purchased a Roberts tile cutter and modified it so that it would produce 3-inch x 12-inch wide strips and then 3-inch squares. It took a full winter to roll out and cut the tiles.

The cut tiles had a problem: they were not flat. They still had the radius contour of the roll. I experimented and found that if I took a stack of tiles, placed them between two oak blocks and squeezed them together with an 8-inch C-clamp and then baked them in our kitchen oven for two hours at 200 degrees that they would flatten out.

The next challenge was the adhesive. Most modern floor adhesives are water-based and do not hold up long term when subjected to high temperatures (closed car in summer) or low temperatures (below freezing in winter). After some searching, I found a 2-part urethane tile adhesive that would meet the task. So, now I was ready to start laying tile.

I started in the men's room doorway since the tile had to transition into the hallway and put down the first batch of tile. I was admiring my first installed batch when the next problem arrived: the urethane adhesive is exothermic when it cures. As it warmed up, the curve of the tile returned. I spent the next couple of hours continuously rolling down the tiles to keep them flat. I needed a better solution.

I finally found the solution... **BEER.**

A 12 ounce beer bottle full of water weighs 1.2 pounds and is the correct size to place in the middle of a tile to hold it flat while it cures. I also home brew beer so I had a ready supply of empty bottles and new caps. I was sure that the CSX employees who saw me loading cases of "beer" into the car thought I was going to have a heck of a party. The beer bottles filled with water worked great, but I was limited to being able to only install fifty-six tiles at a time. That was as far as I could reach to place the bottles on the tiles.

The long hallway showing the concrete floor and the bottles holding down the new tiles.

The completed tiles in the men's room.

Window Sash Restoration

The windows have been in the sun and elements since they were built/rebuilt in 1931 (eighty-eight years). There are two colors of paint evident on the outside: the original color Pullman green, which was painted over with Wabash red after the car was sold to the Wabash in 1953.

Window exterior

The inside of the window is not much better. There are multiple levels of paint over the top of the finished mahogany. There are one to two coats of MoW green covered by white paint.

This particular window sash had dry rot damage that needed to be repaired

Here is a close-up of the exterior paint at the top of the sash.

The first step in the restoration is to remove the paint from each side. I chose mechanical abrasion as the least detrimental to the wood surface. Here is the inside of the sash with the bare wood exposed.

The sash exterior has had the paint removed except for the rounded area next to the glass. The amount of dried and damaged wood is more evident.

This photo shows the damaged area of the sash that will need to be repaired. It looks pretty sad.

The next step is to remove the inside quarter round and the glass pane. The quarter round is too brittle to save and is discarded. If the window pane has no cracks, it will be cleaned and reused.

All of the damaged wood was removed. I used an oscillating multi-tool and chisels. The area to be repaired includes both the inside and outside surfaces. The sashes are assembled with mortise and tenon joints. The remains of the original tenon are shown and will be used.

Here is another photo that shows the inside of the sash for the same area

The next bit of "fun" is to cut a piece of replacement material to fit into the location. I like to use old American mahogany if I have material available. In this case, I am using a piece of Philippine mahogany that has been cut and shaped to fit over the remaining window material.

The wood is held in place using only wood glue, like the original windows. The finished material has been inserted into the sash.

The outside surface of the sash showing the same repair.

The next step is to remove the paint from the rounded window edge. I use a quarter-inch wide chisel to slowly pick and scrape all of the paint from the surface and then sand using a sanding sponge (shown). The flat surfaces are all sanded with a palm sander to determine what other surface defects need attention. Any surface dents, scratches or holes on the sash exterior surface should have any paint or dry-rotted wood removed using a chisel. The bottom edge usually has dry-rot, and the easiest solution is to cut ¼ inch from the bottom. The bottom is angled at 7 degrees toward the outside. I also trimmed the width of the windows to a standard dimension of 28 1/8 inches. Pullman originally trimmed the windows to match each opening which varied from 28 inches to 28 ½ inches.

The next step is the start of preservation. The sash exterior surface will be painted Pullman green and it needs a surface that is holds paint better than bare wood. I used West Systems Marine Epoxy for this task. The exterior wood surface is coated with epoxy, which is allowed to soak in and dry. After it dries, if there are still areas that are not glossy, those areas get coated again. And again.

West Systems epoxy coated over the window on the exterior

Letting the epoxy soak into the wood, it turns the surface into plastic. The dried epoxy can be sanded with 100 and 150 grit sand paper to make it smooth. Any of the imperfections that were dug out with a chisel can now be repaired using the same epoxy with a glass powder filler. It will take several coats before everything is smooth. Afterwards, I masked the interior surface and sprayed light gray automotive primer over the exterior surface.

Window exterior after primer

Now it is time to start working on the interior of the sash. The first step is to use the chisels to remove any of the residual window putty that held the glass. I also use the palm sander to sand the interior surfaces.

Window interior after sanding

Of course, there is also damage to the interior of the sash. This photo shows a chipped area along with a scratch that is still filled with paint.

Residual damage examples

I use Famowood mahogany filler to repair holes and surfaces. This stuff stains almost the same color as the original mahogany. It is petroleum based and dries quickly, so I occasionally add a splash of MEK (methyl ethyl ketone) to keep it workable. Notice that I also filled the screw holes for the handles so that the screw threads will have something to bite into when installed.

Wood filler applied.

This sash required some additional chisel work to be done to carve out for the sash latching handle. The handles were previously restored using full strength ammonia to remove the original paint and then two coats of primer, two coats of gold paint and two coats of lacquer.

Sash latch mounting area and restored latch

Now, it is finally ready for some finish work. I used Minwax Red Mahogany stain because it penetrates into the wood well and matches the original wood finish. I followed the stain with eight coats of Minwax Wipe-On Poly Gloss coating.

Stained window interior

After the Poly hardened, I masked the inside surface of the sash and brush painted the exterior primed surface with Imron 2-part urethane paint. The Imron levels out sufficiently, when applied with a good brush, so that there will be no brush marks.

Imron applied to the exterior of the window

Now it is time to put the window pane back into the sash and install the handles. I use a bead of Lexel adhesive caulk on the wood surface before inserting the glass. The pane is held in place using quarter-round moulding. I made new quarter round moulding using additional Philippine mahogany that was stained and finished beforehand. The two sash handles have been installed using new no. 6 oval head slotted screws.

The window restoration is complete

The finished product took about 3 weeks to complete, not including the quarter round fabrication and the handle restoration. The Villa Real has a total of thirty-eight windows. I was usually working on four windows at the same time but in different stages of restoration.

Faux Woodgrain Finish

During the paint removal process in the section area, I discovered that layers of old paint applied over one of the berths could be removed when the temperature was cold and expose the original woodgrain finish underneath. The paint could be picked off a little at a time, using a knife point, when the temperature was below freezing. It took a couple of winters to be able to fully expose the berth.

The original faux woodgrain finish exposed

I did a lot of internet searching for information on faux woodgraining techniques and materials and came away with very few answers. My wife and I were on a driving trip to New England and were passing near the Whippany Railway Museum in New Jersey. We stopped so that I could shoot a few railfan photos. She stayed in the car to wait for a "few minutes." As I wandered around the grounds, I met the only museum volunteer who was there that afternoon. He was working on restoring a caboose interior. As we talked, I learned that he did faux woodgraining for a living. I spent about one and a half hours picking his brain on techniques, materials, and pitfalls. I learned enough information that I was ready to start experimenting. Of course, my wife was very "pleased" with my extended absence.

After the old paint was removed from the upper berths, I applied a coat of Rust-Oleum red oxide rusty metal primer followed by a grey automotive primer coat. The first layer of coloring is actually pumpkin orange oil-based paint. That was the recommendation from the expert and confirmed by the interior paint samples I cross sectioned. I applied the paint with a brush since the brush marks help with the graining effect.

Pumpkin orange oil-based paint applied to the upper berths.

The wood grain color is actually wood stain applied to the surface. A penetrating stain like Minwax will not work. The stain has to have some thickness almost like sour cream. I purchased several different brands and colors of stain and quickly determined that one layer of stain or even two layers of stain were insufficient. I also determined that it would require layers of different color stains to give a rich wood look. After some experimentation, I found that the best combination was two coats of Zar Products Walnut stain followed by one coat of Varathane Carrington stain. The application tool recommended was the big surprise. The super-cheap chip brush (so bad they will not even call it a paint brush) is the tool. The streaking that it leaves can be worked to look like woodgrain. There are several orientations of pattern for the woodgrain. I marked the outline of the pattern with a pencil and masked the areas with delicate-surface-release painters tape.

The final Carrington stain on the borders with masking and graining in process in the center

The finished woodgraining stain

Several days were required to complete each berth. Temperature was important: if too hot, the stain would dry quicker than it could be worked to complete the graining. The walnut stain had a maximum temperature of 70 degrees and the Carrington was limited to only 60 degrees. So, it was definitely a cool season project.

The next task was to reproduce the lines and graphics. The original berth surface shows a fairly intricate design of grain directions as well as the striping. I found an automotive pinstriping tape supplier (finessepinstriping.com) that had two stripe masking tape that was nearly identical in line width and spacing to the original Villa Real stripes. This is a pressure-sensitive tape with a cover layer that peels away and then paint is applied between the remaining stripes of tape. After some practice, I was able to apply the tape in a straight line and the tape did not damage the stain when removed.

Finesse Pinstriping also supplied the cans of paint. The paint was applied with small artist brushes. The graphics were created by DIY Lettering using my artwork.

Corner graphics on the upper berths

Graphics and pinstriping applied

I had already started applying the graphics when I realized that I had a scaling issue with the artwork that I had sent to DIY Lettering. I decided to continue rather than try and remove the graphics I had already applied and risk damage to the woodgraining.

Finished woodgraining with stripes and graphics.

The Porter Call Box

The porter call box is a device that is mounted high on the hallway wall just outside of the men's room. It has letters and numbers to indicate the various locations within the car such as the berths, bedrooms, restrooms, and vestibule doors. A push button is located in each of those areas that is used to summon the porter. Pressing the button causes an electromagnet to move an arrow to point to the location and also activates a buzzer to get the porter's attention. The porter can then look at the box and tell where the summons came from.

When the Villa Real was converted to a MoW wrecker foreman's car by Wabash in June of 1957, part of that conversion included removing the porter call box from the car and throwing it on the scrap heap. Rick Gillum, a Wabash employee, rescued the box, took it home, and kept it all the years that the car was in MoW service. After Norfolk Southern sold the car at auction in Birmingham, Alabama, he offered the porter call box to John Baker (the car's original purchaser), who gladly accepted.

I received the porter call box in 1995 and added it to the very large pile of artifacts to be restored and did not touch it again until 2020.

Multiple layers of paint had been applied to the porter call box over the years and the steel mounting brackets were well rusted. The face of the lettered surface was heavily cracked and the lettering was in bad shape. However, the inside mechanism was made up of brass and steel parts that were in excellent shape.

Restoration started with a thorough cleaning. The steel brackets were removed and stripped to bare metal. Two coats of oil-based primer were applied followed by the brown enamel paint. The wooden frame was sanded to bare wood and any damaged surfaces were repaired with stainable wood filler. Surprisingly, the wood was poplar rather than mahogany.

The porter call box with the cover glass removed

The lettering and lettering surface were another challenge. The lettering board had been made before the assembly of the arrows, which were soldered into place. I decided that removing the arrows was not going to end well, so I prepared to do the work in, around, and under the arrows. I found an available font that was identical to the original lettering and had vinyl transfer lettering made. Sanding to remove the original surface was tedious, but eventually accomplished. Like the exterior frame, two coats of oil-base primer were applied followed by gloss enamel paint. Next, masking plates were created that allowed me to apply the gold enamel to the arrows. Then, the lettering was applied and the porter call box was reassembled and installed into its original mounting hole in the hallway.

The restored porter call box installed in the long hallway

Exterior Paint – Round 2

After all of the steel repairs were completed, it was time again to paint the exterior. I divided each side into three segments to make the painting less grueling. The middle segment included the lettering. Before paint could be applied, the surface was lightly sanded to remove any surface oxides and then cleaned to remove the paint dust and any other debris. The next step was to apply the specialty primer in preparation for the Imron paint. Lastly the Imron was applied.

The first two segments have been completed and the center segment remains

Unlike the first time, I painted over the lettering in the center segment with Imron. I then used the visible outline of the original letters to apply masking and then the lettering paint. Unfortunately, Dulux gold was no longer available, and I ended up using a sign painter's imitation gold paint. It was selected for its UV stability and color match.

Sign painter's gold paint applied over the masked lettering.

After the walls were painted, another coat of industrial oil-based black paint was applied to the roof.

The finished exterior paint and lettering

Carpet

The last part of the restoration, like building a house, is the carpet. None of the carpet patterns that Pullman used are available unless a custom carpet is made. I did a lot of on-line searching, but with no luck. I solicited input from a carpet supplier in Raleigh and he suggested Milliken Carpets. Their website did have some patterns that would look like a carpet that could have been used in a Pullman car. I contacted their commercial carpet representative in North Carolina and talked about the application and the size needed. They had a minimum requirement of 250 square feet, which we did meet. The piece that I needed was a 34-foot-long piece from a roll that is 14 feet wide.

The floor in the section area of the car is not conducive to laying carpet. The seat frames are fastened into the concrete floor. The carpet would need to be cut into manageable segments first. I had the carpet delivered to our church, since I had no space available that was big enough to roll it out and cut it. When it arrived, I rolled it out and turned it over to cut it from the back side. The carpet was marked, and each interface was identified, so I could make the patterns line up when installed on the car floor.

There were several of the seat frames where the concrete had cracked and chipped out where the legs were attached. I patched those using the West Systems Epoxy mixed with concrete powder as a filler agent. There were also places in the floor that were worn from years of use and abuse. I sanded the floor where needed and used thinset leveling compound where needed.

I purchased more of the same two-part Urethane adhesive that I had used for the tile floor. I just used a different trowel to apply it. I also bought twenty-four paving blocks to use to hold down each segment of carpet when it was placed onto the adhesive. There were fifteen segments used in the section area and one for each bedroom.

The carpet laying process took a few weeks since I could only apply three segments at a time. The adhesive took three days for a full cure, so I could do two applications per week. The color and pattern of the carpet really compliments the other colors in the car.

The first segments of carpet have been glued in place and weighed down with the paving blocks

The same area with the carpet completed. The pattern match worked very well

Raleigh to Illinois Railway Museum Move

The decision to donate the Villa Real to the Illinois Railway Museum was actually made in 2018, but the donation offer was not formally made until the restoration was nearly complete in 2021. I would make the car available in Raleigh and IRM would be responsible for arranging the transportation from Raleigh to the museum. I would work with the local CSX trainmaster to get the car ready to move on the back of a train.

The first part of preparing the Villa was to ensure that all of the certifications up to date. The car would need new brake valves and hoses, it would need to have a COT&S (clean oil test & stencil) on the main brake cylinder, and it would need a current air brake test and car inspection. I contacted Pittsburgh Airbrake Company to swap the brake valves. I took the old ones off of the car, crated them up and shipped them to PABCO. A couple of weeks later, they returned the crate with the new rebuilt valves. The air hoses came from New York Air Brake Company. It turned out that their factory was in North Carolina, about eighty miles away. I had to buy two pairs to meet their minimum purchase requirement.

Next part was arranging for the COT&S. I contacted Dan Pluta, of Pluta Rail Services, to do the work, but he was booked for six months and he was not able to work on the Villa until August. He also did a car inspection and the current brake test. When we moved the car to Raleigh, I could do the COT&S and the brake test myself. The Federal Railroad Administration later changed some of the rules, and those steps needed to be performed by a certified person.

The third part was the lettering and numbering. The car needed an ULMER number to be identified in the national railway system. IRM facilitated the process, and I was able to choose my own number. I selected 4318, which was the car's number when in Wabash MoW service. So, the car number for transport was IRMX4318. There were several other labels and markings needed. I decided to try the same vinyl labels that they use for automobile advertising. They stick very well, but can be removed using a heat gun.

CSX also sent a car inspector to look at the Villa before they would accept it onto their railroad for movement. At this point, everything passed, and it was almost ready to move. The last thing I had to do was make some steel brackets that would fasten to the buffer plates to hold the end of train (EOT) air-pressure sensor.

The Raleigh trainmaster was having difficulty getting the Villa assigned to a train because of the backlog of freight traffic. COVID had taken a toll on the number of available crews. After 3 weeks, it was finally set up for a move to IRM.

The day of the move, CSX had to bring in a small track gang to replace seven crossties on the siding where the car was parked. On December 29, 2021 the Villa started its journey to the Illinois Railway Museum.

The car traveled from Raleigh to Hamlet, North Carolina; then Greenwood, South Carolina; Chattanooga, Tennessee; Nashville, Tennessee; and on to Chicago, Illinois, on CSX. It arrived in Chicago on Jan 6, 2022.

The Villa sat in the CSX yard in Chicago for two weeks waiting to be interchanged by the Chicago Belt Railway over to Union Pacific. When the Union Pacific received the car, they issued a "bad order" on the car because they did not have a corresponding handling code as CSX for "ship only on the rear of a train." That issue was resolved and the Villa Real was delivered to IRM on January 29, 2022.

COT&S stenciling applied to the battery box

Tie replacement on the siding where the car is parked

Pulling the car off of the siding

Heading south on the first part of the journey

Arrival at the Illinois Railway Museum on January 29, 2022

The Final Result

The Pullman Company took a lot of photographs of their sleeping cars for each production lot. At the beginning of the twentieth century, Pullman sales persons called upon the different railroads to offer their sleeping car service. The photographs were used by the sales persons to show the different types of accommodations that were available to the traveling public. Copies of those Pullman photographs reside in several museums and institutions around the country. I purchased several from eBay. The photographs shown in this chaptter are copies from the Pullman Collection of the Abram Lincoln Presidential Library in Springfield, Illinois, and are reprinted with their permission.

When the restoration of the car interior was complete, I took photographs of the same locations as the Pullman originals.

The completed exterior

Pullman photo – bedroom with hopper

Restored bedroom with hopper

Pullman photo – bedroom couch

Restored bedroom couch

Pullman photo – men's room triple sink

Restored men's room triple sink

Pullman photo – men's room with couch

Restored men's room with couch

Pullman photo – men's room corner and dental sink

Restored men's room corner and dental sink

Pullman photo – men's room couch and settee

Restored men's room couch and settee

Pullman photo – section area

Restored section area

Pullman photo – section area

Restored section area

Pullman photo – ladies' room

Restored ladies' room

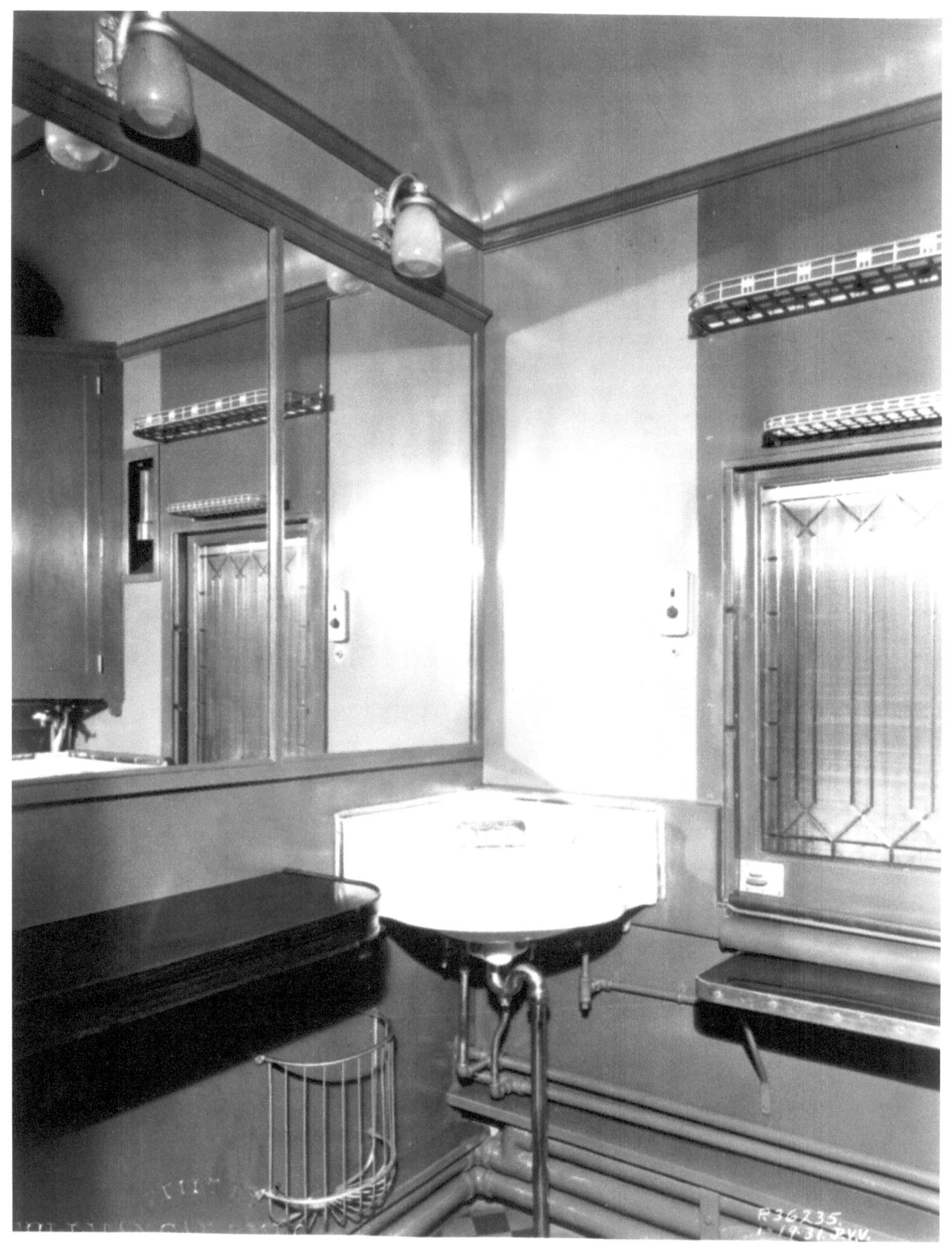
Pullman photo – ladies' room with shelf

Restored ladies' room with shelf

Acknowledgements

I want to thank all of the people who provided information, parts, and assistance in the restoration of the car.

John Baker, Vice-President of Public Relations for Norfolk Southern Railway in Alabama, who had acquired the Villa Real and then sold it to Herman and I.

Larry Thomas and the Terminal Railway Association of St. Louis Historical and Technical Society, Inc. for the research and documentation of the history of the Villa Real. He authored much of the information in the History section of the book. It is reprinted here with his permission.

John McFadden for his assistance and friendship for the twenty-three years that the car was located in Raleigh.

Roger Kramer from the Illinois Railway Museum. I horse traded car parts with him over the years. He was instrumental in getting the car accepted for donation by IRM.

Lois Sauer and Kathryn Cox, my wife and daughter, who would occasionally participate by helping remove the old paint. Lois also helped me with editing the text.

The Abraham Lincoln Presidential Library in Springfield, Missouri, for the use of the Pullman photographs in their collection.

Thomas Sayre for his concrete expertise and help patching the heavyweight floor.

Mike White, CSX trainmaster for the last ten years that the car was in Raleigh. His help was instrumental in arranging to move it out of Raleigh and begin the journey to the Illinois Railway Museum.

North Alabama Railroad Museum for parts donations and allowing me to park the Villa Real on their property for two years.

The Norfolk Western Historical Society for providing a photo of the Villa Real while in maintenance of way service.

Robin and Brent Lewis who made the replacement wheels and bearings available.

Jim Blair and his wife for their interest in the car and their labors to help remove the old interior paint.

James, the homeless guy, who worked with me on the car for two years removing the old paint.

Jan Poff, for his exceptional job of editing this book in order to hide the fact that I am an engineer and not a writer.

www.ingramcontent.com/pod-product-compliance
Lightning Source LLC
Chambersburg PA
CBHW041158290426
44109CB00002B/53